NO GIRLS ALLOWED

ALLOWED

· COOKBOOK FOR MEN ·

GREG FORD

FRONT TABLE BOOKS
AN IMPRINT OF CEDAR FORT, INC.
SPRINGVILLE, UTAH

© 2013 Greg Ford
Photographs © 2013 Greg Ford, except on pp. 9, 17, 18, 20, 31, 34, 35, 40, 42, 46, 51, 57, 68, 71, 84, 93, 114
All rights reserved.

ISBN 13: 978-1-4621-1194-7

Published by Front Table Books, an imprint of Cedar Fort, Inc.
2373 W. 700 S., Springville, UT 84663
Distributed by Cedar Fort, Inc., www.cedarfort.com

   Library of Congress Cataloging-in-Publication Data on file

Cover and page design by Erica Dixon
Cover design © 2013 by Lyle Mortimer
Edited by Aubrey Luddington and Casey J. Winters

Printed in China

10 9 8 7 6 5 4 3 2 1

To my wife, Sue—the source of my inspiration,
and the best cook I know.

CONTENTS

INTRODUCTION

NO GIRLS ALLOWED is a cookbook for men, with great recipes that men like—recipes that are straightforward to make and hard to botch. Each recipe's simple instructions are intended to make it easy for men to get past the initial intimidation of the kitchen and begin making those recipes that they otherwise have to wait for mom, the Mrs., or others to make.

I'VE INCLUDED solid, time-proven recipes with basic ingredients found in most kitchens, recipes that are loved by men, women, and families.

LEARNING HOW TO COOK means you eat better, you eat what you want, and you eat when you want—not to mention it's more economical. It's social and more fun too. With our world's need to improve health, learning how to cook gives you the tools you need to be able to control what you eat.

SOME YEARS AGO, when our son got married, I made a recipe book for him. It was a good time to collect some of the favorite recipes for men from our family and friends and pass them on to him. The book was well received by family members and strangers who bumped into it. And so my writing of recipes began. While some of the recipes survived from my son's cookbook and are included here, many are new and come from the wide array of terrific cooking I have enjoyed during my life.

CHAPTER 1
BREAKFAST

"The only thing I don't eat for breakfast
is lunch and dinner."

—AUTHOR UNKNOWN

OMELETTE

SERVES
2-4

This is the way to start the day!

½ CUP CHOPPED ONION

½ CUP CHOPPED GREEN PEPPER

½ CUP MUSHROOMS

1 TBSP. BUTTER

½ CUP DICED HAM, ½-INCH SQUARES (OR CHOPPED SAUSAGE, CHOPPED BACON, OR OTHER)

1, 2, OR 3 EGGS PER OMELETTE (A 1-EGG OMELETTE IS PLENTY)

1 CUP GRATED CHEDDAR CHEESE

SALT AND PEPPER TO TASTE

SOUR CREAM

AVOCADO SLICES

YOUR FAVORITE SAUCE

· · · DIRECTIONS · · ·

1. SAUTÉ onions, pepper, and mushrooms in butter, until onions are translucent and mushrooms are soft.

2. COOK diced ham (or other meat).

3. DECIDE how many eggs you want in your omelette. Put egg(s) in a bowl and mix so that the white and yolk are blended. Pour the egg into a frying pan heated to medium heat. Roll the pan to spread the egg into an evenly thick oval layer.

4. LET the egg cook until it begins to set. Add the cheese and other chosen "fillings" on one half of the egg. The amount of cheese and fillings are to your taste. Cook until mostly set. When ready, fold the empty half on top of the filling. Cook for an additional minute or so.

5. FLIP omelette and cook for 2-3 minutes. Cook long enough so that the contents are warm, and the cheese is melted.

6. SERVE with salt and pepper and your choice of sour cream, avocado slices, or your favorite sauce.

BELGIAN WAFFLES

There's no waffling about how good these are.

4 EGGS, SEPARATED

½ TSP. VANILLA

3 TBSP. BUTTER, MELTED

1 CUP MILK

1 CUP FLOUR

½ TSP. SALT

2 CUPS STRAWBERRIES, SLICED AND SPRINKLED WITH SUGAR (OPTIONAL)

1 PINT WHIPPING CREAM (OPTIONAL)

· · · DIRECTIONS · · ·

1. BEAT yolks until very light. Add vanilla, butter, and milk and mix. Combine flour and salt and add to egg mixture. Beat well.

2. BEAT egg whites until stiff and fold into batter.

3. COOK on medium-high heat for 3–4 minutes or until light brown. If you're using a non-electric device, be sure to turn the waffle iron over after 30 seconds to 1 minute so the batter runs into the other side of the iron.

4. SERVE with strawberries and whipped cream or other toppings.

SERVES
2-4

BREAKFAST BURRITOS

SERVES
4-6

You can put anything you want in them . . . well, maybe not beets.
But you can have fun with what you put in a burrito.

3 MEDIUM POTATOES (FROZEN HASH BROWNS WORK IN A PINCH, BUT FRESH ARE BETTER)

2 TBSP. BUTTER

½ MEDIUM WHITE ONION

1 TBSP. OLIVE OIL

8 OZ. SMOKED SAUSAGE (BREAKFAST SAUSAGE, HAM, AND BACON WORK TOO)

4 EGGS

8 (8-INCH) FLOUR TORTILLAS

1 CUP SHREDDED MEDIUM CHEDDAR CHEESE

YOUR FAVORITE SALSA

SOUR CREAM TO TASTE (OPTIONAL)

SALT AND PEPPER TO TASTE (OPTIONAL)

· · · DIRECTIONS · · ·

1. CUT potatoes into small/medium pieces. Fry potatoes in butter in a large frying pan over medium heat until done. Potatoes should not be overly crisp. (If you microwave potatoes for a few minutes in advance, they will fry faster.) Set aside.

2. CHOP onion and put into a frying pan with olive oil. Sauté (fry until translucent), about 2 minutes. Set aside.

3. CUT the sausage (or other meat) into bite-size pieces and fry until brown.

4. WHISK eggs and add to sausage. Cook until eggs begin to firm. Add onions and potatoes and continue to cook until eggs are firm but not dry.

5. WHEN eggs are cooked, spoon into warmed tortillas and sprinkle some cheese on top. Add favorite salsa and/or sour cream and salt and pepper to taste. Roll up the burrito and you're set.

6. CONSIDER adding rice, beans, and other favorites to your burrito for extra gusto.

BREAKFAST CROISSANT

This one is so good, it can make you feel guilty. Save calories by not grilling.

BUTTER

HAM SLICE (BEST IF SLICED FROM A PRECOOKED HAM VERSUS SANDWICH SLICES)

VELVEETA CHEESE (CAN USE OTHER CHEESES, BUT VELVEETA IS RECOMMENDED)

1 EGG

1 FRESH CROISSANT

· · · DIRECTIONS · · ·

1. MELT 1 teaspoon butter in a frying pan and cook ham for 2–3 minutes on one side and flip. Put a slice of Velveeta cheese on top and cook until cheese begins to melt. Set aside.

2. FRY egg in butter. Break yolk. Flip egg to set the white and cook yolk. Do not overcook. Set aside.

3. SLICE croissant in half, lengthwise, and butter both sides (on crust side). Make a sandwich of the ham, cheese, and egg, and fry 1–2 minutes at medium heat until cheese begins to ooze. Flip croissant, and cook the other side for 1–2 minutes.

SERVES
1

EGGS

Sooner or later you have to learn how to cook an egg.

People can be very particular about the way they like their eggs cooked. Here are some alternative ways to prepare them. Most recipes are better off if you don't "hover" while cooking them. Eggs are the exception. They cook fast, and can be wrecked in a wink.

FRIED: SOME people are particularly fussy about their fried eggs. They may like them sunny side up (not flipped) but maybe with a set top (white is cooked), or they may like them over easy, where the egg is turned before the white sets. However you prepare them, cook on medium heat and watch them so that they are not overcooked. They cook fairly fast.

POACHED: PUT ½–1 inch or so of water in a frying pan. Heat the water until it begins to boil. Crack an egg into a bowl. Pour the egg from the bowl into the water. Be careful not to get burned. Using a spatula, float water over the top of the egg until cooked to the desired doneness.

SCRAMBLED: CRACK egg into a bowl and whisk. A dash of cream can make them even better. Pour into a frying pan heated low to medium. When the egg begins to set, use a spatula to scramble the egg. When set and still moist, turn off the heat and serve. Remember, low and slow.

HARD-BOILED: PUT eggs in pan. Add cold water to cover. Put a teaspoon of salt in water. Bring to a boil and boil for 6 minutes. Remove from heat and let sit in pan for another 5 minutes. Then run cold water on eggs. (Do not add eggs to boiling water.)

SOFT-BOILED: PUT eggs in pan and cover with cold water. Put a teaspoon of salt in water. Bring to a boil and boil for 4 minutes. Remove from heat, and run cold water on eggs.

QUICHE

Great breakfast with a funny name.

4 TSP. FLOUR

1½ CUPS SHREDDED SWISS CHEESE

1 (9-INCH) UNBAKED PIE CRUST

½ CUP COOKED HAM, DICED

3 EGGS

1 CUP MILK OR CREAM

¼ TSP. SALT

¼ TSP. GROUND DRY MUSTARD

· · · DIRECTIONS · · ·

1. PREHEAT oven to 350°F.

2. IN A medium bowl, mix flour with the grated cheese. Sprinkle mixture into the pie shell. On top of cheese, sprinkle diced ham.

3. IN A medium bowl, combine eggs and milk or cream and then add salt and mustard powder. Beat or whisk until smooth and pour over cheese and ham.

4. BAKE in the preheated oven for 45–50 minutes, or until filling is set and crust is golden brown. Check at 35 minutes to see how it's doing. Cut back on time if it looks like it will burn.

SERVES
4

CREPES

SERVES
4-6

Chalk another one up for the French.

1 CUP PLUS 1 TBSP. FLOUR

3 EGGS

1½ CUPS MILK, DIVIDED

¼ TSP. SALT

3 TBSP. BUTTER

· · · DIRECTIONS · · ·

1. STIR the flour, eggs, ½ cup milk, and salt with a whisk in a bowl or in a blender. Blend well and then add the additional 1 cup milk. Allow the batter to rest 20 minutes. Whisk the melted butter into the mixture just before using.

2. HEAT a 6-inch nonstick pan over medium-high heat. Hold the pan in one hand. Using a small ladle pour out about 2 tablespoons of batter into the pan on the edge where the side meets the bottom. Turn the pan in a circular motion to spread the batter evenly over the bottom of the pan. The amount of batter should just coat the bottom of the pan. Excess should be poured back.

3. COOK the crepe until the edge is brown. Turn the crepe by carefully lifting with a spatula, or, to the delight of your children or guests, you can flip it. To flip, first make sure that the crepe is sliding freely in the pan by shaking it vigorously. Cook the second side for only 10–15 seconds. If overcooked, crepes are dry and brittle.

NOTE: Roll-up (burrito style) with butter, fresh fruit, and jam. Top with whipping cream and some powdered sugar.

GERMAN PANCAKE

This is better than it sounds or looks. It will puff up magnificently while in the oven, to *oohs* and *ahhs* of spectators, and then fall as you take it out.

6 EGGS

1 CUP MILK

1 CUP FLOUR

½ TSP. SALT

2 TBSP. BUTTER OR MARGARINE, MELTED

POWDERED SUGAR

SYRUPS/TOPPINGS OF CHOICE

· · · DIRECTIONS · · ·

1. PLACE the eggs, milk, flour, and salt in a blender. Cover and process until smooth, or whisk until smooth in a medium sized bowl.

2. MELT the butter and place into a 9 × 13 baking dish; add the pancake batter.

3. BAKE uncovered at 400°F for 20 minutes.

4. DUST with powdered sugar and eat right away with your favorite syrups/toppings.

SERVES
8

FRENCH TOAST

This is a great way to use bread that's gone a bit dry—especially French bread.

2 EGGS

½ TSP. CINNAMON

½ CUP MILK

BREAD (SOURDOUGH FRENCH BREAD PREFERRED. OKAY IF OLD AND A BIT DRY.)

SYRUP OR POWDERED SUGAR

· · · DIRECTIONS · · ·

1. BEAT eggs in a bowl. Add cinnamon and milk. Mix.

2. HEAT frying pan to medium. Soak both sides of bread in batter. Fry both sides of bread for 2–3 minutes. Be sure to cook them long enough so that they are not soggy.

3. SERVE with syrup or powdered sugar.

SERVES
2-4

MARY ANNE'S BUTTERMILK PANCAKES

SERVES 2-4

A terrific hand-me-down recipe from Grandmother.

1 TSP. BAKING SODA

½ TSP. SALT

1 TSP. SUGAR

1 CUP FLOUR

1 EGG

1½ CUPS BUTTERMILK

2 TBSP. MELTED BUTTER

· · · DIRECTIONS · · ·

1. MIX baking soda, salt, sugar, and flour in a bowl.

2. BEAT egg and mix with buttermilk. Add buttermilk mixture and melted butter to batter and mix.

3. COOK on medium heat in an oiled or buttered pan. They need to be flipped when bubbles appear on pancake.

PRAGMATIC PANCAKES

While you may have a favorite recipe, sometimes you need to take a more pragmatic/expedient route.

INGREDIENTS & DIRECTIONS

1. KEEP a box of pancake mix on hand. In a pinch, they are extremely easy and fast to make . . . and great to eat.

WHIPPED CREAM

Once you learn how to do this, you're dangerous!

1 PINT WHIPPING CREAM

½ CUP SUGAR

1 TSP. VANILLA

··· DIRECTIONS ···

1. COMBINE ingredients in a mixing bowl and whip at high speed until thick (cold bowl and whisk are best). Be careful not to whip too long or it can turn to butter.

SERVES
4

CHAPTER 2
SANDWICHES

"Ask not what you can do for your country. Ask what's for lunch."

—ORSON WELLES

REUBEN SANDWICH

SERVES
4

Hands down, this is my favorite sandwich.

2 TBSP. MAYONNAISE

1 (16-OZ.) CAN SAUERKRAUT, DRAINED WELL

BUTTER

FRESH SLICED SOURDOUGH FRENCH OR RYE BREAD

10 OZ. SWISS CHEESE

8 OZ. SLICED DELI CORNED BEEF

THOUSAND ISLAND DRESSING (OPTIONAL)

· · · DIRECTIONS · · ·

1. **ADD** mayonnaise to sauerkraut and mix.

2. **BUTTER** one side of each piece of bread.

3. **HEAT** frying pan to medium heat. Preheat sauerkraut in microwave for a minute or so. Put slice of bread, butter side down, in pan. Put slices of cheese on bread first, then meat, then sauerkraut, and some Thousand Island. Put other slice of bread on top, butter side up.

4. **COOK** at low-medium heat. Watch that bread does not burn—it's easy to burn. When bottom side is brown and cheese is melted, flip and cook until the second side is brown. Option: drizzle Thousand Island Dressing on top of sandwich.

NOTE: You can make your own Thousand Island Dressing: Mix together ½ cup mayonnaise, 2 tablespoons ketchup, and 2 teaspoons sweet pickle relish.

MIGHTY MEATBALL SANDWICH

I'm hungry just thinking about this sandwich. And a good meatball will elevate this sandwich to stardom.

1 LOAF SOURDOUGH FRENCH BREAD (OR GRAB ANY GOOD-LOOKING ROLLS, FRESH WHITE BREAD, OR BUNS AT THE BAKERY)

MAYONNAISE

MUSTARD

1 MEDIUM TOMATO, SLICED

½ MEDIUM ONION, SLICED

8 MEDIUM MEATBALLS (PAGE 60)

· · · DIRECTIONS · · ·

1. **SLICE** loaf in half horizontally and then cut into 6-inch lengths.

2. **SPREAD** mayonnaise on both sides of the bread and mustard on one side.

3. **LINE** bottom slice with slices of tomatoes and onion.

4. **PUT** two or three meatballs in sandwich, or cut the meatballs in half and pack them onto bread.

SERVES
1

B.A.T. SANDWICH

Bacon, Avocado, and Tomato—this sandwich is always a winner, especially with fresh tomatoes.

4–6 SLICES OF BACON

1 OR 2 MEDIUM TOMATOES

1 AVOCADO

4 SLICES BREAD (WHITE OR WHEAT)

MAYONNAISE

SALT TO TASTE

FRESH LETTUCE (OPTIONAL)

· · · DIRECTIONS · · ·

1. FRY bacon so that it is crispy but not burnt. Don't ignore it. It can burn quickly. Put the bacon on a paper towel to get rid of excess grease.

2. SLICE the tomato into medium thick slices. Slice the avocado into wedges.

3. TOAST the bread. Put mayonnaise on both slices of bread. Add bacon, avocado, tomatoes and salt to taste.

4. OPTIONAL: Enhance with fresh lettuce.

SERVES
2

SANDWICH WRAP

A wrapped sandwich has a special taste. It also holds a lot of goodies.

SEASONING OF CHOICE: OLIVE OIL, MUSTARD, MAYONNAISE, SALT, PEPPER, AND SO ON

1 (10-INCH) FRESH TORTILLA (OLD TORTILLAS FALL APART)

MEAT OF CHOICE (BEEF, HAM, CHICKEN, TUNA, TURKEY), SLICED THIN

GARNISH OF CHOICE: ONIONS, PICKLES, JALAPEÑOS, PEPPERONCINI, BELL PEPPERS, CHEESE, AVOCADO, AND SO ON

SHREDDED LETTUCE

· · · DIRECTIONS · · ·

1. PUT seasoning on the tortilla. Layer with meat next, followed by the garnish.

2. ADD lettuce as desired.

3. ROLL and eat away.

SERVES
1

TOASTED CHEESE

SERVES
1

It pays off to go the extra mile and toast your sandwich. Great with tomato soup.

CHEESE OF CHOICE: CHEDDAR, JACK, SWISS, OR MIX CHEESES

2 SLICES BREAD (FRENCH, RYE, WHEAT, SOURDOUGH, OR WHITE)

BUTTER

· · · DIRECTIONS · · ·

1. SLICE cheese to cover bread—a generous slice is better than too little.

2. BUTTER one side of each piece of bread. Put the sliced cheese in the middle, with the buttered sides out.

3. HEAT frying pan to medium heat, and cook for 2–3 minutes, until the bottom is brown. Flip and brown the other side, 2–3 minutes, or until the cheese melts.

TUNA/HAM MELT

· · · DIRECTIONS · · ·

1. FOLLOW the same recipe as above, but spread a good amount of tuna or ham slices on top of the cheese before putting on the top piece of bread.

DARRIN'S SPECIAL TUNA FISH SANDWICH

A little extra touch for an old-fashioned sandwich.

1 CAN QUALITY TUNA FISH, DRAINED

2 TBSP. MIRACLE WHIP (CANNOT BE SUBSTITUTED)

1 STALK CELERY, DICED

1 GLOB SWEET PICKLE RELISH

4 SLICES BREAD

1 SMALL TOMATO, SLICED

CHEDDAR CHEESE SLICES (OPTIONAL)

BUTTER (OPTIONAL)

· · · DIRECTIONS · · ·

1. MIX tuna, Miracle Whip, celery, and relish together. Spread the results onto a slice of bread, about a half-inch thick. Add tomato slice. Top off with another slice of bread.

2. OPTIONAL: For a winter version, add a couple slices of cheddar cheese and grill at medium heat for 2–3 minutes per side (butter outside of top and bottom slices of bread).

SERVES
2

BIG HINT FOR A GREAT SANDWICH!

- A good sandwich can be made great by choosing the right kind of bread.

- When you are making a sandwich, take the time to get some good bread. There are many great breads and rolls to try.

- Experiment and you and your family and friends will appreciate the results.

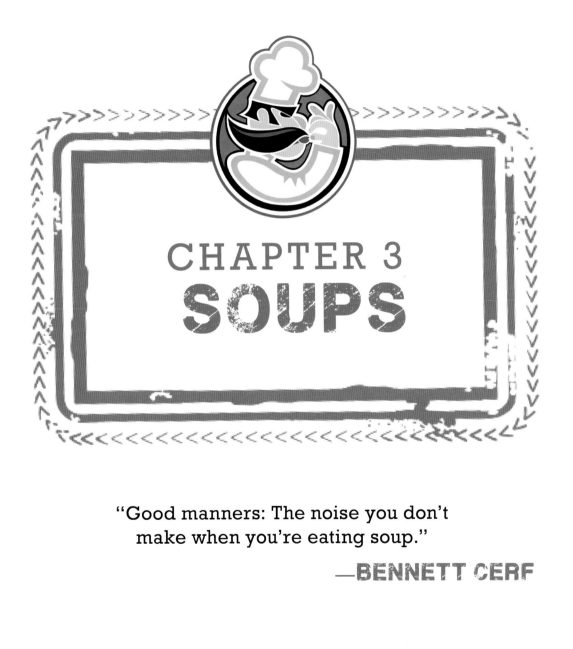

CHAPTER 3
SOUPS

"Good manners: The noise you don't
make when you're eating soup."

—BENNETT CERF

JAMBALAYA

A delicious and filling soup, with some zing.

1 MEDIUM SKIN-LESS, BONE-LESS CHICKEN BREAST, CUT INTO BITE-SIZE PIECES

1 (8-OZ.) PKG. ANDOUILLE SAUSAGE (KIEL-BASA, SMOKED, OR OTHER FIRM SAUSAGE WILL WORK), CUT INTO ¼-INCH SLICES

4 TBSP. BUTTER

2 CLOVES GAR-LIC, CHOPPED

1 MEDIUM ONION, DICED

1 CUP DICED GREEN PEPPER

1 CUP LONG GRAIN RICE

2 (14.5-OZ) CANS DICED SPICY TOMATOES WITH JUICE

1 TBSP. MINCED PARSLEY

½ TSP. THYME

1 TSP. CAJUN SEASONING

1 CUP OKRA (FROZEN OK)

2 CUPS CHICKEN BROTH

1 SMALL BAY LEAF

½ TSP. CAYENNE PEPPER

SALT AND PEP-PER TO TASTE

1 POUND LARGE, UNCOOKED SHRIMP, PEELED AND DEVEINED (OPTIONAL)

···DIRECTIONS···

1. BROWN the chicken and then the sausage in butter in a large pan over medium heat. Remove and set aside.

2. IN the same pan, sauté garlic, onions, and green pepper. When the onions are translucent (3–5 minutes), stir in the rice. Add tomatoes, parsley, thyme, chicken, Cajun seasoning, sausage, okra, and broth. Stir and add bay leaf, cayenne pepper, and salt and pepper.

3. COVER and cook over low heat for 30–45 minutes, or until rice is tender.

4. OPTIONAL: Stir in shrimp, cover, and cook for an additional 5–10 minutes. Shrimp are pink when done.

SERVES 6

DAN'S ONION SOUP

SERVES
6-8

This soup is straight from France.

4–5 WHITE OR YELLOW ONIONS, PEELED AND THINLY SLICED

¼ CUP BUTTER

6 CUPS WATER

6 CUBES BEEF BOUILLON (START WITH 3; ADD ADDITIONAL CUBES AS NEEDED)

1 TSP. WORCESTERSHIRE SAUCE

¼ TSP. SALT

DASH OF PEPPER

1 BAGUETTE

1 CUP SHREDDED SWISS CHEESE (MOZZARELLA OR PROVOLONE WORK TOO)

· · · DIRECTIONS · · ·

1. IN A large saucepan, cook onions in butter (covered) about 10 minutes or until translucent and tender. Add water, bouillon, Worcestershire sauce, salt, and pepper. Bring to a near boil (never boil soup) and simmer for 20 minutes.

2. SLICE baguette into ¼- to ½-inch slices and toast (until crisp) in a toaster or on a cookie sheet.

3. MELT swiss cheese on top of baguette. Options: broil briefly to melt cheese; bake baguette for 1–2 minutes, or until cheese melts; or use a propane torch to melt cheese on top of baguette.

4. LADLE soup into oven-safe bowls. Top with baguette slice and serve.

GRANDDAD'S BEAN SOUP

Granddad frequently made this, and we all loved it.

1 CUP NAVY OR GREAT NORTHERN BEANS

1 HAM HOCK OR LARGE PIECE OF HAM WITHOUT FAT

3 CHICKEN BOUILLON CUBES

1 LARGE ONION, DICED

2 STALKS CELERY, DICED

2 CARROTS, DICED

SALT AND PEPPER TO TASTE

· · · DIRECTIONS · · ·

1. SOAK beans in water overnight.

2. NEXT day, drain beans and add to large pot. Add ham, bouillon cube, onions, celery, carrots, and salt and pepper. Cover with water.

3. BRING to a near boil (bubbles are coming up the side of the pan), and then reduce to a simmer. Cook for approximately 1½ hours or until beans are soft.

4. SALT more to taste. Ham can be removed from the bone and shredded or cubed and then returned to soup.

NOTE: Soup will thicken overnight in the refrigerator. Add water or chicken stock if too thick.

SERVES
6-8

CHEESE AND POTATO SOUP

SERVES 6-8

Cheese is great with everything, especially in soup.

6 MEDIUM POTATOES, PEELED AND CUBED

1 CARROT, CHOPPED

WATER

4 CUPS WHOLE MILK

3 STALKS CELERY, CHOPPED

1 MEDIUM ONION, CHOPPED

1 CUP CHICKEN BROTH

1 CUBE CHICKEN BOUILLON

2 CUPS GRATED CHEDDAR CHEESE

5 STRIPS BACON, CRISP AND CHOPPED

½ CUP BUTTER

½ CUP CHIVES

SALT AND PEPPER

· · · DIRECTIONS · · ·

1. IN A large pot over high heat, cover the potatoes and carrots with water and boil for 10–15 minutes, or until tender (a fork goes in easily). Drain and save potato water in a second pan. Return 2 cups of potato water to the carrots and potatoes plus the milk. Reduce heat to low and simmer.

2. SAUTÉ the celery and onion over medium heat for about 5 minutes, or until onions are translucent.

3. MASH the potatoes and carrots. Transfer the onion and celery mixture to the pot and whisk it in, along with the chicken broth and bouillon.

4. WHILE increasing heat slowly, add the cheese, bacon, and butter, stirring to allow the cheese to melt. Add reserved potato water as necessary to get desired consistency.

5. SALT and pepper to taste.

6. SERVE in bowls, with chives on top.

SPONTANEOUS COMBUSTION SOUP

3 CANS BEEF BROTH

1 CAN WATER

2 CANS SPICY CHOPPED TOMATOES (IF YOU'RE USING RO*TEL TOMATOES, KNOW THAT "ORIGINAL" SPICINESS IS HOT)

1 GREEN JALAPEÑO CHILI PEPPER, SEEDS REMOVED, PEPPER CHOPPED INTO FINE PIECES

10–12 JALAPEÑO MEATBALLS (SEE NOTE IN DIRECTIONS)

1 CAN TOMATO PASTE

1 (12- TO 16-OZ.) PKG. FROZEN CAJUN OR GUMBO VEGETABLES

1 (12- TO 16-OZ.) PKG. FROZEN CORN

½ CUP UNCOOKED RICE (OPTIONAL)

2 TSP. WORCESTERSHIRE SAUCE

· · · DIRECTIONS · · ·

1. MIX all ingredients except Worcestershire sauce in a 5-quart pot.

2. ADD Worcestershire sauce.

3. HEAT until simmering (never boil soup). Let simmer for half an hour.

NOTE: To make your own jalapeño meatballs, add 1 tablespoon diced fresh jalapeños to Meatballs recipe (page 60) after removing seeds and veins.

SERVES
6-8

AUTUMN CHOWDER

I look forward to autumn just to have some more of this soup.

6 SLICES BACON

1 MEDIUM ONION, CHOPPED

2½ CUPS DICED POTATOES

1 CUP SLICED CARROTS

2–3 CUBES CHICKEN BOUILLON (IF KNORR, USE 1)

1 CUP WATER

2 CUPS MILK

2 (16-OZ.) CANS CREAM CORN

1 CAN REGULAR CORN, DRAINED

3 CUPS GRATED MILD CHEDDAR CHEESE

PEPPER TO TASTE

· · · DIRECTIONS · · ·

1. IN A large pan, cook bacon until crisp. Remove bacon, chop, and set aside. Discard grease except 2 tablespoons for onions.

2. SAUTÉ onions in pan for 3–5 minutes or until translucent.

3. ADD potatoes, carrots, bouillon, and water and bring to a simmer for 10–15 minutes, until tender. Watch carefully or the water will burn off. (You can add ½ cup milk if it gets too dry.)

4. ADD milk, corn, cheese, and pepper. Stir constantly on medium-low heat until cheese is melted. Fold in bacon. Be careful not to scorch the soup.

SERVES
6-8

CIOPPINO

SERVES
2-4

A tangy soup that brings back good memories of San Francisco.

2 CUPS FRESH
MUSHROOMS

1 STICK BUTTER

¼ CUP OLIVE OIL

1 LARGE ONION,
CHOPPED

4 CLOVES
GARLIC, MINCED

1 GREEN
BELL PEPPER,
CHOPPED

1 (16-OZ.) CAN
TOMATOES,
DICED

1 (8-OZ.) CAN
TOMATO SAUCE

1 (14.5-OZ.) CAN
CHICKEN BROTH
OR 2 CUPS FISH
STOCK

1 CUP WHITE
GRAPE JUICE

3 TBSP. FINELY
CHOPPED FRESH
PARSLEY

½ TSP. THYME

2 TSP. CHOPPED
FRESH BASIL OR
1½ TSP. DRIED
BASIL

PINCH OF SUGAR

1 LB. COD
FILLETS, CUT
INTO 2-INCH
PIECES (SWAI
FISH IS A GOOD
SUBSTITUTE)

1 LB. WHITE
SHRIMP (21–25
COUNT), PEELED
AND DEVEINED

2 TBSP. LEMON
JUICE

1 LOAF SOUR-
DOUGH FRENCH
BREAD

· · · DIRECTIONS · · ·

1. SAUTÉ mushrooms in 4 tablespoons butter. Set aside.

2. HEAT oil in a very large stockpot. Add onion and sauté until soft. Add garlic and bell pepper; cook 5 minutes. Add tomatoes, tomato sauce, broth or fish stock, grape juice, parsley, thyme, basil, and sugar. Bring to a boil.

3. REDUCE heat and simmer, covered, for 20 minutes. The broth can be made ahead at this point and refrigerated up to 8 hours. Reheat before adding seafood.

4. ADD cod and mushrooms; cover and simmer 5 minutes. Add shrimp, simmer 5 to 10 minutes or until shrimp is pink. Stir in lemon juice. Don't overcook.

5. SERVE with lots of crusty French bread and butter.

CREAM OF MUSHROOM SOUP

Wow! You'll love this. Easy and delicious.

2 (10.75-OZ.) CANS CREAM OF MUSHROOM SOUP

12 OZ. HALF-AND-HALF

1 (7-OZ.) CAN MUSHROOM STEMS AND PIECES

1 TBSP. BUTTER

· · · DIRECTIONS · · ·

1. IN A 2-quart pan, add cream of mushroom soup and stir in half-and-half.

2. STIR in mushrooms and butter.

3. BRING to a simmer, stirring continually (so it won't burn or boil) for 10 minutes.

SERVES
4

CHAPTER 4
SIDES

"If God had intended us to follow recipes,
He wouldn't have given us grandmothers."

—LINDA HENLEY

RICE

Everybody needs to know how to cook a good plate of rice.

1 CUP LONG GRAIN RICE

2 CUPS WATER (2½ CUPS IF USING UNCLE BEN'S RICE)

2 TBSP. BUTTER

1 TBSP. OLIVE OIL

· · · DIRECTIONS · · ·

1. POUR rice into 4-quart pan. Add water and stir so rice is not clumped on the bottom of the pan.

2. BRING the rice to a boil, uncovered, at medium heat.

3. WHEN the rice is boiling, turn the heat down to medium low. Add butter and oil. Cover pan with lid.

4. SIMMER the covered rice for another 20–30 minutes. Stir occasionally to make sure the rice isn't sticking. Add a bit more water if it looks too dry. When done, fluff with a fork and serve hot.

SERVES
4–5

PASTA NOODLES

SERVES
6-8

Like rice, you need to know how to cook good noodles.

1 LB. PASTA (1–1½ CUPS UNCOOKED PASTA PER PORTION)

2 TSP. SALT

· · · DIRECTIONS · · ·

1. FILL a 4-quart pot halfway with water and put on stove at high.

2. ONCE the water is boiling, add salt to water and carefully place the noodles into the water. Using a spoon, push all of the noodles underwater.

3. STIR frequently to prevent sticking.

4. AFTER about 6 minutes take one noodle out and check if it's ready. The noodles should be firm to the bite (*al dente*) but without a hard center. As necessary, continue cooking and testing until the noodles are done to your taste. Different-sized pasta have different cooking times. For example, angel-hair cooks quickly, while fettuccine takes much longer. (As a last resort, check the box for directions. However the *al dente* test is the final arbiter.)

5. DRAIN the noodles in a colander in the sink. Don't rinse the pasta unless the pasta will be used for a cold dish, such as a salad. If so, then you may want to rinse.

6. EAT right away.

PETITE PEAS

Peas go with almost any meal.

1 (12- TO 16-OZ.) PKG. FROZEN
PETITE PEAS (A CAN OF PEAS
IS *NOT* A GOOD SUBSTITUTE)

1½–2 TBSP. BUTTER

½ TSP. DILL

PINCH OF SALT

· · ·**DIRECTIONS**· · ·

1. COOK peas at medium heat in a 1-quart pan for 3–6 minutes. They don't need to be cooked, only heated through.

2. DRAIN peas. Add butter, sprinkle with dill, and serve.

SERVES
6-8

CAROTTES À L'ÉTOUFFÉE

This is an easy way to get your vitamins and nutrients. You may be able to see better too.

5–6 MEDIUM CARROTS, CUT LENGTHWISE IN QUARTERS, AND 2-INCH LENGTHS

1 TSP. DILL

3 TBSP. BUTTER

WATER

· · · DIRECTIONS · · ·

1. PLACE carrots, dill, and 1 tablespoon butter in a saucepan over very low heat and cover with a tight-fitting lid. Add water to cover carrots.

2. COOK until the carrots are tender. Depending on the size, this will take 15–20 minutes. Watch the water level—it can evaporate before the carrots are done, and the carrots will burn.

3. REMOVE the lid and increase the heat to allow the remaining moisture to evaporate. Coat carrots in the remaining butter by gently tossing.

SERVES
6-8

ASHLEY'S GREEN BEANS

If you have someone who won't eat their green beans, try this.

2 (14.5-OZ.) CANS FRENCH-CUT GREEN BEANS, DRAINED

1 TBSP. BUTTER, MELTED

1 (10.75-OZ.) CAN CREAM OF MUSHROOM SOUP

4 OZ. FRENCH-FRIED ONIONS

· · · DIRECTIONS · · ·

1. PREHEAT oven to 350°F.

2. COMBINE beans, melted butter, and cream of mushroom soup in 8 × 8 baking pan.

3. PUT in the oven for about 20 minutes.

4. WHEN ready to serve, stir in onions or spread on top.

SERVES
6-8

OVEN-ROASTED POTATOES

Most of these will be stolen before dinner.

6 POTATOES

2 TBSP. OLIVE OIL

1 (1.25-OZ.) PKG. DRY ONION SOUP MIX

· · · DIRECTIONS · · ·

1. PREHEAT oven to 400°F. Cut potatoes into bite-size pieces, peels optional.

2. PUT potatoes on cookie sheet lined with foil and spray with nonstick spray.

3. DRIZZLE olive oil on top of potatoes. Stir. Shake soup mix over potatoes and stir again.

4. COOK potatoes in oven for 20 minutes. Move potatoes around with a spatula to keep from sticking. Cook an additional 20 minutes until brown and crisp.

NOTE: For the soup mix, you can substitute salt and pepper, seasoned salt, and garlic. You can also substitute other vegetables for potatoes, such as mushrooms, zucchini, and so on.

SERVES
4-6

BAKED BEANS

You will not believe how good these are.

2 (28-OZ.) CANS PORK AND BEANS

¾ CUP BROWN SUGAR

1½ TSP. YELLOW MUSTARD

⅔ CUP CATSUP

· · ·DIRECTIONS· · ·

1. MIX ingredients together in a baking pot.

2. COOK in the oven at 325°F for 3–4 hours. Stir every hour. Great the first day, better the second.

SERVES
8-10

FAMILY POTATOES

While it may sound a bit morbid, these are commonly called *funeral potatoes*. They are for sure at every funeral meal and every other food-eating gathering in Utah because they are quick and good!

5 POTATOES (OR 2 PKGS. FROZEN HASH BROWNS, THAWED)

1 MEDIUM ONION, CHOPPED

1 (10.75-OZ.) CAN CREAM OF CHICKEN SOUP

1 CUP SOUR CREAM

¼ CUP MELTED BUTTER

2 CUPS GRATED CHEESE

1 CUP BREAD CRUMBS OR CRUSHED CORN FLAKES (OPTIONAL, BUT TASTY)

· · · DIRECTIONS · · ·

1. CUT potatoes in quarters. Boil for 25–30 minutes. Done when fork goes in easily. When cool, peel and grate.

2. SAUTÉ onions. Cook until onions are translucent.

3. PREHEAT oven to 350°F. Combine grated potatoes (or hash browns) with cream of chicken soup, sour cream, onions, butter, and grated cheese in 9 × 13 baking pan.

4. SPRINKLE bread crumbs (or crushed corn flakes) on top and bake for 30–45 minutes.

SERVES 6-8

NUKED CORN ON THE COB

Quick and easy . . . and good!

FRESH CORN ON THE COB
(PEEK INSIDE THE HUSK AND
LOOK FOR SMALL, YOUNG
CORN KERNELS—NOT BIG,
TOUGH, YELLOW KERNELS)

· · · DIRECTIONS · · ·

1. CUT off the tassel end, above the cob. Moisten the cob in the sink.

2. PUT in the microwave for 3½ minutes.

3. WITH a hot pad, take the ear back to the sink and remove the husk under cold, running water.

SERVES
1

CHAPTER 5
SALADS

"Knowledge is knowing a tomato is a fruit;
wisdom is knowing not to put it in a fruit salad."

—AUTHOR UNKNOWN

SHRIMP LOUIE

A great, easy-to-make salad.

8 SPEARS ASPARAGUS (NOT CANNED)

1 HEAD LETTUCE

1 LB. COOKED AND DEVEINED FRESH SHRIMP (IF YOU WANT TO ANNOY YOUR FRIENDS, LEAVE THE TAILS ON. TO REMOVE THE TAILS, PINCH THE SHRIMP AT THE TAIL AND REMOVE TAIL.)

8 STRIPS BACON, CRISPY

2 MEDIUM TOMATOES, CHOPPED

4 HARD-BOILED EGGS (PAGE 8), SLICED

2 CARROTS, CHOPPED

1 AVOCADO, SLICED

1 MEDIUM ONION, CHOPPED

1 (16-OZ.) PKG. SHREDDED CHEESE

THOUSAND ISLAND DRESSING TO TASTE

· · · DIRECTIONS · · ·

1. SIMMER asparagus for 5 minutes in a frying pan with bottom covered with ½ inch water. Don't overcook.

2. REMOVE damaged or wilting leaves from head of lettuce. Chop lettuce into ½-inch slices, or tear by hand into eatable pieces.

3. PUT a serving of lettuce in the center of a plate and a serving of shrimp on top. Arrange the rest of ingredients, except dressing, to suit your eye.

4. POUR on dressing. (If you don't have Thousand Island Dressing, mix together the following: 1 cup mayonnaise, ½ cup ketchup, 2–3 tablespoons sweet pickle relish, 1 teaspoon lemon juice, and salt and pepper to taste.)

SERVES
4

CAESAR SALAD

The king of salads.

1 HEAD ROMAINE
LETTUCE, CHOPPED WITH
A KNIFE OR SHREDDED BY
HAND

½ CUP FRESH GRATED
PARMESAN CHEESE

1 CUP CROUTONS

½ CUP SLICED RED ONION

1 CUP CAESAR SALAD
DRESSING (HIGHLY
RECOMMENDED)

SALT AND PEPPER TO TASTE

· · · DIRECTIONS · · ·

1. MIX first five ingredients together in a salad bowl.
Add salt and pepper.

NOTE: Most lettuce should be torn by hand—doing
so slows the edges from turning brown.

SERVES
6-8

GARDEN SALAD

SERVES
6-8

Let your imagination run wild. It's hard to ruin a garden salad . . . but it *is* possible.

1 HEAD ROMAINE OR ICEBERG LETTUCE, TORN OR SHREDDED BY HAND

2 MEDIUM TOMATOES, DICED

1 MEDIUM ONION, SLICED OR CHOPPED

SALAD DRESSING OF CHOICE

SALT AND PEPPER TO TASTE (RESTAURANT-GRADE PEPPER IS WORTH IT)

· · · DIRECTIONS · · ·

1. COMBINE lettuce, tomatoes, and onions in a bowl.

2. APPLY dressing. (Too much hides the flavor of the ingredients, and too little can make everything a bit chewy, so be careful.)

3. MIX together and add salt and pepper.

NOTE: Many extra things go well in a salad—take a look at salad bars with all of the choices that are offered (sliced hard-boiled egg, real bacon bits, olives, artichoke hearts, fresh cooked asparagus, pepperoncini, chopped celery, apple slices, pear slices, parmesan cheese, blue cheese crumbles, beets, grated carrots, avocado slices, croutons, parsley, cilantro, peas, and more). Use your judgment on combinations and amounts . . . don't go crazy.

WINTER SALAD

When tomatoes are not available—or for something different—oranges make a good substitute.

½ HEAD ROMAINE OR BIBB LETTUCE

2 ORANGES

½ MEDIUM RED ONION

ITALIAN DRESSING

· · · DIRECTIONS · · ·

1. SHRED lettuce.

2. PEEL and cut oranges into slices.

3. CUT onion into slices.

4. MIX ingredients in a salad bowl, dress with Italian dressing, and eat.

SERVES
4-6

GREEN BEAN AND MANDARIN ORANGE SALAD

This is a tasty salad that's easy to make.

1 (15-OZ.) CAN CUT WHITE WAX BEANS

1 (15-OZ.) CAN CUT GREEN BEANS

1 (11-OZ.) CAN MANDARIN ORANGES

⅓ CUP RED ONION, CHOPPED (ADJUST TO TASTE)

½ CUP ITALIAN DRESSING

3 TBSP. SUGAR

SALT AND PEPPER TO TASTE

· · · **DIRECTIONS** · · ·

1. DRAIN beans and oranges.

2. PLACE beans and onions in a large bowl. Mix sugar into dressing and pour over salad. Add salt and pepper and toss gently. Blend oranges carefully so that oranges are not mangled. Best well chilled—the longer the better.

SERVES
6-8

CARROT AND RAISIN SALAD

My mother made this when we were kids, and I still love it.

¾ CUP MAYONNAISE

6 CARROTS, PEELED AND GRATED

½ CUP RAISINS

2 TSP. SUGAR

¾ CUP PINEAPPLE TIDBITS, DRAINED

· · · DIRECTIONS · · ·

1. IN A salad bowl, mix the mayonnaise, grated carrots, raisins, sugar, and pineapple tidbits. Cover and chill for an hour in refrigerator.

SERVES
6-8

POTATO SALAD

It should be illegal to have a picnic without this salad, especially when it's so easy to make.

8 POTATOES

1 MEDIUM RED ONION, CHOPPED

6 SWEET PICKLES, CHOPPED (CAN USE ½ CUP PICKLE RELISH)

3 STALKS CELERY, DICED

1 TBSP. YELLOW MUSTARD, PLUS MORE TO TASTE

2 TSP. SUGAR

3 TBSP. SOUR CREAM

1½ CUPS MAYONNAISE (IT MAY BE NECESSARY TO ADD ADDITIONAL TO KEEP THE SALAD MOIST)

SALT AND PEPPER TO TASTE

· · · DIRECTIONS · · ·

1. BOIL potatoes until a knife enters easily into potato. Don't overcook. Allow potatoes to cool and then peel and cut into bite-size pieces.

2. IN A large bowl, mix onion, pickles, celery, mustard, and sugar. Add the potatoes. Smear the sour cream on top, and then carefully stir it in—don't mash the potatoes. Add mayonnaise and stir it in. Add salt and pepper. Allow to sit for at least half an hour or more to allow flavors to blend. May be better the second day.

SERVES
6-8

BAKED POTATO BAR

An often overlooked meal that people love and that is easy to make.

4–6 LARGE POTATOES

1 CUP SOUR CREAM

½ CUP BUTTER

2 TOMATOES, CHOPPED

6 GREEN ONIONS, CHOPPED

5 PIECES OF BACON, COOKED AND CHOPPED

1½ CUPS GRATED CHEESE

2 CUPS MUSHROOMS, SAUTÉED

1 CUP CANNED OLIVES

· · · DIRECTIONS · · ·

1. SCRUB potatoes, poke several holes in them with a fork (keeps them from exploding), and bake until done, about 1 hour at 350°F (when you squeeze them, they will give when done, and a fork goes in easily). Don't overcook.

2. CUT each potato down the middle, but not all the way. Squeeze to open.

3. FILL with favorite stuff . . . don't skimp.

SERVES
4-6

KISS OF STRAWBERRY JELL-O

This salad from yesteryear is so good and refreshing.

1 (10-OZ.) PKG. FROZEN STRAWBERRIES

1 (10-OZ.) PKG. FROZEN RASPBERRIES

1 (6-OZ.) PKG. RED RASPBERRY OR STRAWBERRY JELL-O

1½ CUPS BOILING WATER

1 (1 LB., 4-OZ.) CAN CRUSHED PINEAPPLE

· · · DIRECTIONS · · ·

1. ALLOW berries to thaw.

2. IN A large bowl, dissolve Jell-O completely in boiling water.

3. ADD raspberries, strawberries, and crushed pineapple. Stir.

4. POUR into a 9 × 13 dish and refrigerate.

SERVES
6-8

WAY KOOL JELL-O

Try this to see how *kool* it is.

1 (3-OZ.) PKG. LIME JELL-O

1 PINT COTTAGE CHEESE

1 CAN CRUSHED PINEAP-
PLE (OR FRUIT COCKTAIL),
DRAINED

1 (8-OZ.) PKG. COOL WHIP

· · · DIRECTIONS · · ·

1. IN A large bowl, combine Jell-O, cottage cheese, pineapple, and Cool Whip.

2. REFRIGERATE to let set.

SERVES
6-8

CHAPTER 6
MEAT

"Red meat is not bad for you. Now
blue-green meat, that's bad for you!"

—TOMMY SMOTHERS

HUNGRY ON SUNDAY STEW

Nothing hits the spot like stew on a Sunday afternoon. This recipe can also be done in a slow cooker.

2 LBS. BEEF STEW MEAT, CUT INTO CHUNKS

3 TBSP. FLOUR

2 (10.75-OZ.) CANS CREAM OF MUSHROOM SOUP

2 CUPS WATER

1 PKG. ONION SOUP MIX

3 BEEF BOUILLON CUBES

1 TBSP. WORCESTERSHIRE SAUCE

SALT AND PEPPER TO TASTE

4 POTATOES, CUT INTO QUARTERS, SKINS ON

2 ONIONS, PEELED AND CUT INTO QUARTERS

3 MEDIUM CARROTS, CUT IN HALF LENGTHWISE, THEN CUT INTO 2-INCH PIECES

· · · DIRECTIONS · · ·

1. PLACE beef stew meat in a Dutch/French oven on stove burner. Toss flour evenly across the top of meat. Turn heat on medium-high and sear until meat is brown. Stir to brown evenly.

2. PREHEAT oven to 250°F. Cover meat with mushroom soup and water. Stir in onion soup mix. Add bouillon and Worcestershire sauce. Salt and pepper. Cover with aluminum foil and transfer to oven. Cook for 6 hours.

3. AFTER 4 hours, add potatoes, onions, and carrots. Add water as necessary, and re-cover with aluminum foil. Cook for remaining 2 hours.

SERVES
6-8

BEEF ROAST

The west was won on this.

1 (4- TO 5-LB.) ROUND ROAST

SALT AND PEPPER

SEASONINGS OF CHOICE

VEGETABLES OF CHOICE
(POTATOES, ONIONS, CARROTS, AND SO ON)

· · · **DIRECTIONS** · · ·

1. PLACE the round roast fat side up in a roasting pan. Season the meat as desired using salt, pepper, and other seasonings of choice.

2. PREHEAT oven to 350°F, and place the roast inside. Cook until the roast reaches 145°F (medium rare), 150°F to 155°F (medium), or 160°F or above (well done). A rule of thumb is to cook it 20 minutes for every pound. However, the thermometer trumps the rule of thumb.

3. ADD vegetables at any time, but at least 1 hour before finished.

SERVES
4-6

CHICKEN-FRIED STEAK

Sometimes overlooked, this is a great meal.

2 LBS. CUBE STEAK (TENDERIZED TOP ROUND OR TOP SIRLOIN)

½ CUP MILK

2 EGGS

2 CUPS FLOUR, DIVIDED

1½ TSP. SALT

1 TSP. PEPPER

½ TSP. OREGANO

2 TBSP. STEAK SEASONING SALT

¼ CUP VEGETABLE OIL

· · · **DIRECTIONS** · · ·

1. TENDERIZE cube steak with a tenderizing mallet, if necessary. Most cube steak comes tenderized.

2. IN A medium bowl, mix milk with eggs. Stir thoroughly.

3. IN A second bowl, mix 1 cup flour with salt, pepper, oregano, and steak seasoning salt.

4. PUT vegetable oil in large frying pan and heat to medium-high. Put remaining flour in bowl and dip both sides of cube steak in flour and then in egg-milk mixture. Roll in seasoned flour mixture, generously coating both sides Place steak into frying pan and brown on both sides, approximately 5–7 minutes per side. Remove from pan while steak is still medium rare in middle.

SERVES
4-6

GRANDDAD'S MEATLOAF

This recipe is a well-justified family tradition.

1½ LBS. GROUND BEEF

½ LB. GROUND SAUSAGE

1 (10.75-OZ.) CAN CREAM OF MUSHROOM SOUP, DIVIDED

1 EGG

¾ CUP BREAD CRUMBS

1 LARGE ONION, DICED

1 BEEF BOUILLON CUBE, DISSOLVED IN 1 CUP WATER

· · · DIRECTIONS · · ·

1. MIX all ingredients together except ½ can cream of mushroom soup.

2. BAKE in greased bread pan at 350°F for 45–60 minutes.

3. WHEN finished, pour off juice and add the remaining ½ can soup to the juice for gravy.

SERVES
6-8

MEATBALLS

It's handy to be able to make meatballs. They can go into many other recipes.

1½ LBS. GROUND BEEF

½ LB. GROUND SPICY SAUSAGE

1 PACKET SPAGHETTI SEASONING

1 EGG

¾ CUP BREAD CRUMBS

1 MEDIUM ONION, CHOPPED

1 CAN TOMATO SAUCE

· · · DIRECTIONS · · ·

1. MIX all ingredients together in a mixing bowl. Make meatballs to preferred size, golf ball size is generally adequate. Don't pack the meatball.

2. PUT sheet of aluminum foil on bottom of cookie sheet. Lightly oil the foil. Place meatballs on the sheet and bake for 15–20 minutes at 350°F.

SERVES
6-8

PORK ROAST

A delicious meal with great leftovers.

1 (4- TO 5-LB.) BONELESS PORK LOIN ROAST

1 TSP. SALT

1 TSP. GROUND BLACK PEPPER

½ TSP. GARLIC POWDER

2 ONIONS, CHOPPED

1½ CUPS WATER, DIVIDED

· · · DIRECTIONS · · ·

1. PREHEAT oven to 350°F.

2. SEASON outside of roast with spices. Place roast with onions in roasting pan. Pour ¼ cup water into pan and cover.

3. ROAST pork for 30 minutes covered. Uncover, and turn meat over. Continue to roast uncovered, checking temperature every 30 minutes; add additional liquid if pan runs dry. Roast uncovered until internal temperature reaches 145°F, or for about 20–30 minutes per pound. When it reaches temperature, it must also rest for at least 3–5 minutes. If it's at temperature, it may be slightly pink, but it will be done.

SERVES
6-8

POT ROAST

Another Sunday tradition.

1 (4- TO 5-LB.) CHUCK ROAST

1 (10.75-OZ.) CAN CREAM OF MUSHROOM SOUP

1 PKG. ONION SOUP

3 BEEF BOUILLON CUBES

WATER

6 CARROTS

6 POTATOES

2 ONIONS

SALT AND PEPPER TO TASTE

· · · **DIRECTIONS** · · ·

1. PLACE chuck roast in a deep casserole dish with lid. Cover with the mushroom soup, and sprinkle package of onion soup on top. Add bouillon cubes and water to ⅓ height of roast. Don't cover.

2. CUT carrots in half, and then into 2-inch lengths. Cut potatoes and onions in quarters. Put vegetables around the edges of the roast. Salt and pepper to taste.

3. PLACE dish, covered, in oven and bake for 3 hours at 325°F.

SERVES
6-8

HAMBURGER STROGANOFF

Treat yourself to some simple luxury with this recipe.

½ MEDIUM ONION, CHOPPED

2 TBSP. BUTTER OR MARGARINE

1 LB. GROUND BEEF (YOU CAN UPGRADE AND USE THIN SLICES OF STEAK, ROAST, AND SO ON)

1 (10.75-OZ.) CAN CREAM OF MUSHROOM SOUP

½ TSP. GARLIC POWDER

1 BEEF BOUILLON CUBE

SALT AND PEPPER TO TASTE

DASH OF WORCESTERSHIRE SAUCE

½ CUP SOUR CREAM

· · · DIRECTIONS · · ·

1. IN A large frying pan, sauté onions in butter or margarine until translucent, 2–3 minutes.

2. IN THE same pan, cook ground beef until done at least medium.

3. STIR in cream of mushroom soup, garlic powder, beef bouillon cube, salt and pepper, and Worcestershire sauce.

4. SIMMER for 10 minutes. Stir in sour cream. Serve over noodles (page 35), rice (page 34), or baked potato.

SERVES
4-6

HAM

Every once in a while, you need a good ham dinner.

1 (5-LB.) BONE-IN HAM
(PRESLICED HAMS WILL DRY
OUT FASTER THAN A BONE-IN
HAM)

⅓ CUP YELLOW MUSTARD

⅓ CUP MAPLE SYRUP

2 TBSP. BROWN SUGAR

2 TSP. ONION POWDER

· · · DIRECTIONS · · ·

1. PREHEAT oven to 325°F. Place the ham in a shallow roasting pan with flat side down, fat side up.

2. IF the ham doesn't come with a prepackaged glaze, then in a small bowl mix together the mustard, maple syrup, brown sugar, and onion powder. Coat the ham entirely with the glaze using a spoon or brush.

3. COVER the ham with foil, and roast until heated through. Uncover for the last half an hour. Most hams come precooked, and so this amounts to a heating process vs. cooking. However, it should reach 140°F (145°F for partially or uncooked hams). Estimated cooking time is approximately 20 minutes per pound.

4. WHEN cooked, let it rest for about 3 minutes to allow the temperature to even out and for the juices to come to the surface.

SERVES
6-8

TURKEY

Turkey is not only delicious, it's also good for you. It's well worth getting over the initial intimidation of cooking one.

1. TO prepare the turkey for roasting, first remove the turkey neck and giblets. Some great recipes use them, but you won't need them for this recipe.

2. TO stuff the bird, follow instructions on the stuffing mix. Never stuff a turkey the night before. Stuff only just before cooking, or cook the stuffing/dressing separately.

3. BRUSH the skin with melted butter or oil.

4. PLACE the bird in a roasting pan and into a preheated 325°F oven. Bake until the skin is a light golden color (30–45 minutes) and then cover loosely with a foil tent.

5. COOKING times will vary depending on how big the turkey is and whether it's stuffed or not. A stuffed turkey will take 15–20 minutes per pound, with the shorter time per pound for a bigger turkey. An unstuffed turkey will take 10–15 minutes per pound. Check online for more exact cooking times.

6. DURING the last 45 minutes of baking, remove the foil tent to brown the skin. Baste. Also, cut between the thigh and the rib cage to allow better cooking of the dark meat on the thigh.

7. TURKEYS generally come with a pop-out indicator to indicate when they are done, and they usually work—be patient. You can and should also insert a meat thermometer into the thickest part of the breast, avoiding touching the bone. It's done when it reaches 165°F. You should also check the thigh and stuffing, which should also be at 165°F.

8. RELY on the thermometer, but you can expect at least 2–3 hours for even a small turkey.

9. LET the turkey rest for 20 minutes after it's done before carving.

GRAVY: MILK, BEEF, TURKEY

You can make gravy from any meat—roast turkey, chicken, beef, pork, and more—to pour over sliced beef, pork chops, mashed potatoes, stuffing, roast turkey, chicken, and more.

4 TBSP. DRIPPINGS
(OR BUTTER)

3 TBSP. FLOUR

1 CUP BROTH, PLUS MORE TO
GET DESIRED THICKNESS (OR
OTHER LIQUID)

SALT AND PEPPER TO TASTE

2 BEEF BOUILLON CUBES

MUSHROOMS (OPTIONAL)

SERVES
6-8

· · · DIRECTIONS · · ·

1. REMOVE the meat from the cooking pan and set aside to rest. Leave the drippings in the pan. If you're baking in a glass dish, pour juice into a stovetop pan.

2. ADD broth to drippings and bring to a boil. Scrape goodies from bottom and sides of pan with a wooden spoon or spatula. Whisk until the drippings have been totally dissolved for a smooth gravy.

3. WHISK flour into boiling drippings. Continue to whisk as gravy thickens.

4. ADD more broth or water to get to desired volume and thickness. The liquid used can be broth, milk, or heavy cream, depending on how rich and thick you want the gravy. Add bouillon. The longer the gravy boils, the more it thickens. Keep whisking until it's done. Remember that it will thicken as it cools.

DIRECTIONS (CONTINUED)

5. THE drippings provide some seasoning. Add more to suit your taste.

6. MUSHROOMS can be added for additional texture and flavor.

7. LUMPS and clumps can be avoided by diligent whisking.

BUFFALO WINGS

A treat that's easy to do.

2 CUPS BARBECUE SAUCE

1 TBSP. HOT SAUCE

DASH OF CAYENNE PEPPER

2 LBS. CHICKEN WINGETTES

DRESSING OF CHOICE
(HOMEMADE IS BEST)

· · · DIRECTIONS · · ·

1. POUR barbecue sauce in a bowl. Mix in hot sauce and cayenne pepper.

2. PREHEAT oven to 375°F. Cover bottom of a baking dish in aluminum foil.

3. IF you have full wings, cut off tips and cut wings at joints.

4. SPREAD sauce on both sides of wingettes and place in dish. Cover (aluminum foil works) and place in oven for 30 minutes. At 30 minutes, remove cover, baste in sauce, and cook for 30 more minutes, basting once more after 15 minutes.

5. DIP in dressing of choice and grab the napkins.

SERVES
10 - 12

CHAPTER 7
CHILI &
CASSEROLES

"I just wish I had time for one more bowl of chili."

—dying words of **KIT CARSON**

UNCLE BUD'S THIRD-PLACE CHILI

Every once in a while, even the best judges make mistakes.
This is blue-ribbon chili.

3 LBS. TOP ROUND STEAK, CUT INTO ½-INCH CUBES

2 TBSP. BUTTER

3 TBSP. CHILI POWDER, DIVIDED

3 ONIONS, DICED

½ GREEN BELL PEPPER, DICED

4 CLOVES GARLIC, MINCED

6 OZ. APPLE CIDER

1 (16-OZ.) CAN V8 JUICE SPIKED WITH 1 TSP. TABASCO SAUCE

1 (16-OZ.) CAN TOMATO SAUCE

1 (6-OZ.) CAN DICED MILD GREEN CHILIES

2 TSP. CUMIN

CAYENNE PEPPER TO TASTE

· · · DIRECTIONS · · ·

1. IN A large frying pan, brown meat in butter with 1 tablespoon chili powder. Set aside.

2. IN THE same pan used for cooking the meat, sauté onions, bell pepper, and garlic until onions are translucent and pepper and garlic are limp, about 2–3 minutes.

3. IN A mixing bowl, mix remaining chili powder in apple cider. Combine with spiked V8 juice, tomato sauce, chilies, cumin, and cayenne pepper. Blend.

4. COMBINE all ingredients in large frying pan and simmer 30–45 minutes.

NOTE: This is a recipe for competition chili and is made to be cooked within a time limit. This is terrific chili, but to get meat that melts in your mouth, you need to cook it longer. Cooking it in a slow cooker for 6 hours or more will add to this already terrific chili.

GRANDDAD'S CHILI

We loved Granddad's recipes, especially this one.

2 LBS. GROUND BEEF

2 (15-OZ.) CANS RED BEANS

1 LARGE ONION, DICED

1 (15-OZ.) CAN DICED TOMATOES

1 (8-OZ.) CAN TOMATO SAUCE

2 TSP. CHILI POWDER

SALT AND PEPPER TO TASTE

· · · **DIRECTIONS** · · ·

1. **IN A** large frying pan, fry ground beef until brown.

2. **ADD** rest of ingredients and simmer for 20 minutes.

SERVES
4-6

QUICK PORK CHILI

This recipe is terrific and easy to make.

1 MEDIUM ONION

2 TBSP. OLIVE OIL

1–2 LBS. LEFTOVER PORK ROAST

1 (12-OZ.) BOTTLE MEDIUM SALSA

SALT AND PEPPER TO TASTE

· · · DIRECTIONS · · ·

1. IN A frying pan, sauté onion in olive oil until translucent, 2–3 minutes.

2. CUT roast into 1-inch-or-so squares and fry until brown.

3. ADD medium salsa and salt and pepper. Simmer for 20 minutes.

SERVES 4-6

TOO-HUNGRY-TO-COOK CHILI

When you're hungry and it's halftime, you can make yourself an extra special bowl of chili in a snap.

1 (15-OZ.) CAN CHILI

1-2 HOT DOGS CHOPPED INTO 1-INCH SEGMENTS (HIGHER QUALITY HOT DOGS TASTE BEST)

SHREDDED CHEDDAR CHEESE

· · · DIRECTIONS · · ·

1. MIX ingredients in a medium bowl and microwave, covered with a paper towel to avoid splatter.

SERVES
1-2

CORNBREAD

It's not really a chili meal without cornbread.

½ CUP BUTTER

½ CUP SUGAR

½ TSP. BAKING SODA

2 TBSP. CORNMEAL

2 CUPS BISQUICK

2 EGGS, WHISKED

¾ CUP MILK

½ TSP. VANILLA

· · · **DIRECTIONS** · · ·

1. MELT butter in microwave (50–60 seconds).

2. COMBINE sugar, baking soda, cornmeal, and Bisquick in a mixing bowl.

3. IN A separate bowl mix eggs, milk, and vanilla.

4. ADD egg mixture to Bisquick mixture and stir. Add melted butter and stir.

5. POUR mixture into a baking pan and bake at 325°F for 30 minutes. Check for doneness by sticking a toothpick in the bread. If it comes out clean, the bread is done.

SERVES
4-6

DAN'S FAVORITE CASSEROLE

Our son is always ready for this.

1 (14-OZ.) PKG. PEPPERIDGE FARMS STUFFING (BLUE PACKAGE)

½ CUP BUTTER

2 COOKED CHICKEN BREASTS (THIGHS WORK TOO), CUT INTO BITE-SIZE PIECES

1 (10.75-OZ.) CAN CREAM OF MUSHROOM SOUP

1 (10.75-OZ.) CAN CREAM OF CHICKEN SOUP

1 CUP SOUR CREAM

½ CUP MAYONNAISE

1 (4-OZ.) JAR PIMENTOS

1 (7-OZ.) CAN MUSHROOM STEMS & PIECES, DRAINED

1 (12-OZ.) PKG. FROZEN PETITE PEAS (NO SUBSTITUTION)

· · · DIRECTIONS · · ·

1. MELT butter in 9 × 13 baking dish. Pour stuffing mix in baking dish and stir. Save ⅓ and set aside.

2. MIX remaining ingredients in a bowl and pour over stuffing mix.

3. SPRINKLE remaining stuffing mix on top, cover with aluminum foil, and bake for 20–25 minutes at 350°F.

SERVES
6-8

PASTA PAZOO

SERVES
6-8

Many of my married friends in college asked for this recipe to induce labor . . . no guarantees.

4 BONELESS COOKED CHICKEN BREASTS, CUBED

1 (10.75-OZ.) CAN CREAM CHICKEN SOUP

1 (10.75-OZ.) CAN CREAM OF MUSHROOM SOUP

1 CUP MILK

1 ONION, CHOPPED

1 (15-OZ.) CAN CHILI CON CARNE, WITHOUT BEANS

2 (4-OZ.) CANS DICED GREEN CHILIES

BUTTER

3 TBSP. CHICKEN BROTH

12 CORN TORTILLAS, CUT INTO 1- TO 1½-INCH STRIPS

½ LB. SHREDDED CHEDDAR CHEESE

SALT AND PEPPER TO TASTE

· · · DIRECTIONS · · ·

1. MIX chicken, soups, milk, onion, chili con carne, and chilies in a bowl.

2. GREASE a 9 × 11 casserole dish well with butter. Spread chicken broth evenly on the bottom.

3. COVER bottom evenly with ⅓ of tortilla strips and add layer of ½ of chicken-sauce mixture. Repeat for a second layer. Finish by putting remaining strips on top as well as cheese. Salt and pepper to taste.

4. COVER with foil and refrigerate for 24 hours.

5. BAKE at 325°F for 30–40 minutes. It's done when it bubbles.

NOTE: There is no official pasta in this recipe, but the name has a long tradition. Broadly speaking, tortillas could be considered a Mexican pasta.

CHAPTER 8
MEXICAN

"My doctor told me to stop having intimate dinners for four. Unless there are three other people."

—ORSON WELLES

BURRITOS

Make them the way you like them . . . and as big as you want.

1 LB. GROUND BEEF

¼ CUP CHOPPED ONION

1 (1.25-OZ.) PACKET TACO SEASONING

WATER

1 (15-OZ.) CAN REFRIED BEANS

¼ CUP MILD TACO SAUCE

8 (8-INCH) FLOUR TORTILLAS

SHREDDED CHEDDAR CHEESE

SOUR CREAM

CHOPPED TOMATOES (OPTIONAL)

SHREDDED LETTUCE (OPTIONAL)

· · · DIRECTIONS · · ·

1. BROWN ground beef along with chopped onions. Drain. Add packet of taco seasoning and water as directed on package. Bring to a boil. Reduce heat and stir in refried beans and mild taco sauce. Bring to a boil and remove from heat.

2. IN A frying pan, heat tortillas until warm and soft. Put hamburger-bean mixture on each tortilla. Cover with cheddar cheese and sour cream. Add tomatoes, shredded lettuce, and additional taco sauce if desired and roll up.

SERVES
4–6

CHILI RELLENOS CASSEROLE

Easy to make and great to eat.

1½ CUPS GRATED JACK CHEESE

1½ CUPS GRATED CHEDDAR CHEESE

1 (7-OZ.) CAN WHOLE GREEN CHILIES

8 EGGS

1½ CUPS MILK

1 TBSP. FLOUR

½ TSP. CUMIN

½ TSP. CHILI POWDER

SALT AND PEPPER TO TASTE

· · · DIRECTIONS · · ·

1. MIX cheeses.

2. SPREAD half of the cheese into a greased 9 × 13 pan.

3. SLICE chilies lengthwise along one side and open. Lay flat in a single layer over the cheese.

4. SPRINKLE remaining cheese over chilies.

5. IN A separate bowl, combine remaining ingredients. Mix well. Pour over cheese and chilies.

6. BAKE, covered, at 350°F for 35–45 minutes, uncovered for the last 10 minutes. Eggs should be set (firm) and golden brown.

SERVES
6-8

ENCHILADAS

**SERVES
6-8**

Enchilada should mean hot, as in good, and these enchiladas are hot.

4 SKINLESS, BONELESS CHICKEN BREASTS

1 ONION, CHOPPED

½ PINT SOUR CREAM

1¾ CUPS SHREDDED CHEDDAR CHEESE, DIVIDED

1 TBSP. DRIED PARSLEY

½ TSP. DRIED OREGANO

½ TSP. GROUND BLACK PEPPER

½ TSP. SALT (OPTIONAL)

1 (15-OZ.) CAN TOMATO SAUCE

½ CUP WATER

1 TBSP. CHILI POWDER

⅓ CUP CHOPPED GREEN BELL PEPPERS

1 CLOVE GARLIC, MINCED

8 (10-INCH) FLOUR TORTILLAS

1½ CUPS ENCHILADA SAUCE

· · · DIRECTIONS · · ·

1. PREHEAT oven to 350°F.

2. COOK chicken in a frying pan until white (no longer pink) and juices run clear. Pour off fat. Cube the chicken and return it to the pan.

3. ADD the onion, sour cream, cheddar cheese (reserve ¾ cup), parsley, oregano, and ground black pepper. Heat until cheese melts. Stir in salt, tomato sauce, water, chili powder, green pepper, and garlic.

4. DIVIDE the mixture evenly between the 8 tortillas. Ladle a small amount of the enchilada sauce on top of the mixture and roll. Place in a 9 × 13 inch baking dish. Cover with enchilada sauce and remaining ¾ cup Cheddar cheese. Bake uncovered for 20 minutes. Cool for 15 minutes before serving.

REFRIED BEANS

What's a Mexican meal without refried beans?

1 (1-LB., 15-OZ.) CAN REFRIED BEANS

1 CUP GRATED CHEDDAR CHEESE

· · · DIRECTIONS · · ·

1. PREHEAT oven to 350°F.

2. SPRAY bottom of 8 × 8 glassware bowl with nonstick cooking spray. Spread refried beans evenly across the bottom.

3. SPRINKLE grated cheese evenly on top of the beans.

4. COOK for 20 minutes.

SERVES
4-6

SPANISH RICE

This is subtle but delicious.

1 CUP LONG GRAIN RICE

1 (15-OZ.) CAN MEXICAN
STEWED TOMATOES (USE
JUICE TOO)

2 CHICKEN BOUILLON CUBES

¾ TSP. CUMIN

½ TSP. SALT

3 TBSP. BUTTER

2¼ CUPS WATER

½ TSP. CHILI POWER

· · · DIRECTIONS · · ·

1. MIX ingredients in a 2-quart saucepan. Bring to boil and cook for 20 minutes.

SERVES
6-8

TAMALES RAPIDOS

Tamales are a delicacy in Mexico, but they are a little difficult to make. There are at least two good ways to get tamales. First, find a good Mexican store or restaurant that sells them, or, second, buy them frozen at your grocery store. In all cases, you gotta have them.

1 (6-COUNT) PKG. FROZEN TAMALES

1½ CUPS RED SAUCE (PAGE 84), GREEN SAUCE (PAGE 85), OR ORANGE SAUCE (PAGE 86)

· · · DIRECTIONS · · ·

1. COOK tamales per instructions on package. You can cook in a microwave or in a double boiler.

2. SERVE with sauce of choice.

SERVES
4-6

RED SAUCE

1 (10-OZ.) CAN MILD RO*TEL DICED TOMATOES AND GREEN CHILIES (PREFERRED), WITH LIQUID, OR OTHER CAN OF SPICED DICED TOMATOES

2 (8-OZ.) CANS TOMATO SAUCE

1 TSP. SALT

2 GARLIC CLOVES, CRUSHED

2 TBSP. OLIVE OIL

2 TBSP. ORANGE JUICE OR 1 TBSP. FROZEN CONCENTRATE

¾ TSP. SUGAR

· · · DIRECTIONS · · ·

1. SIMMER ingredients together for about 20 minutes, stirring regularly.

SERVES
6-8

GREEN SAUCE

1 LARGE ONION, CHOPPED

1 LARGE BELL PEPPER, CHOPPED

10 TOMATILLOS, FRESH OR FROM A CAN

1 JALAPEÑO, MINCED, VEINS AND SEEDS REMOVED

1 TBSP. LIME JUICE

1 BUNCH CILANTRO

SOUR CREAM

· · · DIRECTIONS · · ·

1. SAUTÉ onions and bell peppers. When onions are translucent and peppers are soft, add tomatillos and jalapeno. Remove husks from tomatillos (if fresh) and cook until tomatillos are soft.

2. PUT in blender and blend. Pour blended contents in bowl, and stir in lime juice and cilantro (stems removed).

3. STIR in sour cream to desired consistency.

SERVES
4-6

ORANGE SAUCE

1 MEDIUM ONION, DICED

1 TSP. SALT

2 CLOVES GARLIC, CRUSHED

1 TSP. GROUND OREGANO

1 TSP. GROUND CUMIN

¾ TSP. SUGAR

1 CUP CHOPPED GREEN CHILI PEPPERS

3 CUPS TOMATO JUICE

½ CUP SOUR CREAM

· · · DIRECTIONS · · ·

1. SAUTÉ the onions until soft with all spices and green chili peppers. Add tomato juice and simmer for 20 minutes. Pour mixture into a blender. Add sour cream and blend until smooth.

SERVES
6-8

CHAPTER 9
BARBECUE

"The only time to eat diet food is while
you're waiting for the steak to cook."

—JULIA CHILD

SUGGESTED GROUND RULES FOR BARBECUING

1. CLEAN your grill before barbecuing. Do not leave bristles that can attach to food and be eaten.

2. WHILE cooking, use tongs and/or a spatula, not forks—don't stab meat because it lets the juices out.

3. WHEN possible, use a propane barbecue. It's easier to start and stop, there's less mess, and the heat level can be controlled.

4. INDIRECT cooking is cooking near the flame (or coals) but not over it. Direct cooking is cooking directly over the flame/coals. Generally, cook meat by the indirect method. Finish by using the direct. It's hard to cook meat over a flame without burning it.

5. TURN your meat only once. Flip-flopping dries the meat.

6. HAVE a good digital thermometer. It will save you grief.

7. MINIMUM cooking temperatures are 145°F for whole meats, 160°F for ground meats, and 165°F for poultry. See the United States Department of Agriculture website for requirements.

8. CLEAN your grill after barbecuing. Do not leave bristles. The grill is easier to clean while it's hot.

BRISKET

The king of Texas barbecue.

1 (5-LB.) BRISKET, TRIMMED

BRISKET RUB, OR MAKE YOUR OWN WITH:

4 TBSP. CHILI POWDER

½ TSP. CAYENNE PEPPER

1½ TSP. BLACK PEPPER

2½ TSP. GARLIC POWDER

1 TSP. ONION POWDER

½ TSP. PAPRIKA

LIQUID SMOKE (OPTIONAL)

· · · DIRECTIONS · · ·

1. PIERCE the meat several times with a fork, and coat the meat generously with the rub. Wrap the meat in foil and make sure it is sealed well.

2. PLACE wrapped brisket in a 9 × 13 baking pan and cook in a 250°F oven for about 7 hours. Serve with your favorite barbecue sauce. (Yes, this is listed in the barbecue section since it is a famous barbecue dish. However, it's a well-kept secret that you can cook it more easily in your oven.) To properly barbecue a brisket, you need a smoker.

SERVES
6-8

BARBECUE NEW YORK STEAK

You deserve this luxury occasionally.

SALT AND PEPPER

2 (6-OZ.) NEW YORK STEAKS
(IT'S WORTH IT TO SPLURGE
OCCASIONALLY—T-BONE,
PORTERHOUSE, AND RIB EYE
ARE ALSO GOOD CHOICES)

SPICY STEAK SEASONINGS
(OPTIONAL)

WORCESTERSHIRE SAUCE
(OPTIONAL)

· · · DIRECTIONS · · ·

1. SALT and pepper both sides of steak.

2. COOK via indirect method, and finish with direct (page 88). While salt and pepper are sufficient, optional steak seasonings and Worcestershire sauce can be used at this point.

3. THE steak is medium rare when juices appear on the top of the steak. Temperature should be at least 145°F. Be aware of the thickness of the steak—thin steaks cook quicker.

SERVES
1

RIBS ON THE GRILL

Ribs are great and are simple to cook, but you have a problem: ribs taste best when they are cooked slowly for a long time. Grills do not do this well. It doesn't take very long for ribs to get burned and ruined on a grill, unless you follow the directions below.

2–3 LBS. RIBS
(TAKE YOUR PICK: PORK RIBS, BEEF RIBS, AND SO ON)

BARBECUE SAUCE OF CHOICE

· · · DIRECTIONS · · ·

1. PRECOOK ribs by boiling them for about 20 minutes.

2. MARINATE ribs in your favorite barbecue sauce for an hour.

3. COOK ribs on the grill using the indirect method (page 88), basting them every 15 minutes with barbecue sauce. Ribs are done when the meat begins to separate from the bone.

SERVES
4–6

RIBS IN THE OVEN

While this lacks the romance of the barbecue, it makes great ribs.

2–3 LBS. RIBS
(TAKE YOUR PICK: PORK RIBS, BEEF RIBS, AND SO ON)

SALT AND PEPPER

GARLIC POWDER

BARBECUE SAUCE OF CHOICE

· · · DIRECTIONS · · ·

1. LINE baking pan with aluminum foil.

2. SEASON ribs with salt and pepper and a little garlic powder on both sides. Place ribs in pan, meaty side up. Bake in oven at 350°F for 30–45 minutes.

3. BASTE the roasted ribs with barbecue sauce and bake at 350°F for an additional 45–60 minutes or until the ribs are tender, basting every 15 minutes or as needed. The meat will begin to separate from the rib when done.

SERVES
4-6

BARBECUE SALMON

SERVES 4

This is more heart-friendly than most meats.

DON'S SPECIAL SECRET SAUCE:

¼ CUP SOFT MARGARINE

¼ CUP MAYONNAISE

½ TSP. DRIED DILL TO TASTE

1 TSP. LEMON JUICE

4 SALMON FILLETS (SOCKEYE, KING, OR COHO PREFERRED)

· · · DIRECTIONS · · ·

1. MIX the margarine and mayonnaise together in a mixing bowl. When thoroughly mixed, add the dill and lemon juice and stir thoroughly.

2. PLACE a fillet of fresh salmon (with the skin still on it) skin-side down on a hot grill. With a barbecue brush, paint the secret sauce on the flesh side of the fillet, being careful to cover the edges. The sauce should cover the fish thoroughly, but if you use too much it will liquefy and drain off onto the coals and create a fire.

3. BARBECUE salmon for 4–7 minutes—actual time depends on the heat of the coals and the thickness of the fillet. The salmon should be served a bit rare. Overcooking salmon makes it tough and reduces its succulent melt-in-your-mouth qualities.

BARBECUE SAUSAGE

This is a personal favorite.

SAUSAGE LINKS OF CHOICE

· · · DIRECTIONS · · ·

1. COOK indirectly (page 88) until the sausage is so hot it's ready to split or has split. This requires rolling it every few minutes to make sure it heats evenly and doesn't burn. Don't blacken completely, although it isn't bad with some black. Overcooking makes it dry.

SERVES
1

SAUSAGE WRAP

In Texas they eat these for breakfast . . . and lunch and dinner for that matter.

HIGH-GRADE HOTDOG OR SAUSAGE LINK

FLOUR TORTILLA WITH A DIAMETER LESS THAN THE LENGTH OF SAUSAGE (IT'S BETTER TO HAVE THE SAUSAGE STICKING OUT OF THE TORTILLA THAN TO HAVE TOO MUCH TORTILLA)

YELLOW MUSTARD

· · · DIRECTIONS · · ·

1. GRILL sausage until sweating and on the verge of splitting (not totally blackened).

2. PUT sausage in tortilla, put a line of mustard along sausage, and wrap sausage in the tortilla.

ALTERNATIVE: Microwave sausage until beginning to sweat. Wrap sausage in flour tortilla and microwave for an additional 20 seconds. Unwrap carefully and add mustard. Rewrap.

SERVES
1

BARBECUE VEGGIES

Barbecued veggies are a great addition to your meal.

VEGETABLES OF CHOICE (MOST VEGETABLES DO WELL WHEN BARBECUED, LIKE CORN, TOMATOES, GREEN PEPPERS, MUSHROOMS, ONIONS, ASPARAGUS, AND SO ON. SOME, LIKE CUCUMBERS, CELERY, AND MOST LEAFY GREENS, DON'T BARBECUE WELL BECAUSE OF THEIR HIGH WATER CONTENT.)

VEGETABLE GRILL BASKET OR ALUMINUM FOIL

COOKING OIL AND MARINADES (MARINADES CAN INCLUDE ITALIAN DRESSING, HERBS AND/OR BUTTER, SESAME SEED OIL, AND ON AND ON)

· · · DIRECTIONS · · ·

1. MARINADE or brush vegetables to help vegetables cook better and to make them less likely to stick.

2. CUT vegetables into slices, which will allow them to cook better.

3. PUT marinated vegetables in a grill basket or on aluminum foil or directly on the grill. The basket or foil will help keep the smaller slices from falling into the fire. However, putting them in foil will reduce the amount of smoke flavor. Lightly coat the basket, foil, or grill with cooking oil before cooking.

4. VEGETABLES cook relatively fast, but different vegetables will cook for different lengths of time. Don't let them burn.

5. FOR barbecuing corn: Soak corn on the cob with husk for an hour or so, and cook directly on the grill until husk is charred.

LONESOME BOB'S BARBECUE SAUCE

We've always wondered why Bob was lonesome.

1 CUP KETCHUP

¼ CUP WATER

¼ CUP VINEGAR

¼ CUP ORANGE JUICE

⅓ CUP BROWN SUGAR

3 TBSP. OLIVE OIL

2 TBSP. PAPRIKA

1 TBSP. CHILI POWDER

1 TSP. GARLIC POWDER

½ TSP. CAYENNE PEPPER

· · ·DIRECTIONS· · ·

1. MIX ingredients thoroughly in a saucepan. Simmer for 15 minutes, until thickened.

"ALREADY WENT TO THE STORE BUT FORGOT THE BARBECUE SAUCE" SAUCE

How many times do we forget to buy barbecue sauce at the store? But you *can* make your own terrific barbecue sauce.

1 (8-OZ.) CAN TOMATO SAUCE OR 1 CUP KETCHUP

⅓ CUP BROWN SUGAR

¼ CUP ORANGE JUICE

¼ TSP. CRUSHED RED PEPPER

DASH OF WORCESTERSHIRE SAUCE

PINCH OF GARLIC POWDER

SALT AND PEPPER TO TASTE

· · · DIRECTIONS · · ·

1. MIX ingredients thoroughly in a saucepan. Simmer for 10–20 minutes, until thickened.

CHAPTER 10
INTERNATIONAL

"The trouble with eating Italian food is that
five or six days later you're hungry again."

—GEORGE MILLER

INDIAN CHICKEN AND RICE TOUT DE SUITE

If you're not a fan of Indian food, this may persuade you.

1 CUP RICE

2½ CUPS WATER

1 CARROT, PEELED AND DICED

3 CHICKEN BOUILLON CUBES

3 TBSP. BUTTER

2 BONELESS CHICKEN BREASTS

1 (15-OZ.) JAR TIKKA MASALA SAUCE

2 TBSP. HEAVY CREAM

· · · DIRECTIONS · · ·

1. PUT rice in pan with water. Add carrots, bouillon cubes, and butter. Cook rice per directions on page 34.

2. COOK chicken in medium frying pan until meat turns white (about 8 minutes per side) and then dice. (If you start with frozen chicken, allow to partially thaw, and then dice.)

3. ADD masala sauce and heavy cream. Heat to simmering and simmer for 20 minutes.

4. SERVE chicken over rice.

SERVES
2-4

SAUERKRAUT AUS DEUTSCHLAND

You may think you don't like sauerkraut, but try this.

3 LBS. PICNIC SHOULDER PORK ROAST

2 (32-OZ.) JARS SAUERKRAUT

2 GREEN APPLES

1 TSP. PEPPERCORNS

1 ONION, DICED

½ CUP BROWN SUGAR

1 TBSP. CARAWAY SEEDS

4–6 LINKS PREMIUM HOTDOGS OR SAUSAGE, CUT INTO 2-INCH LENGTHS

4–6 POTATOES

¼–½ TSP SALT

4 TBSP. BUTTER

¼–½ CUP MILK

· · · DIRECTIONS · · ·

1. PLACE roast in bottom of slow cooker. Pour undrained sauerkraut into pot.

2. SLICE apples and add to pot along with peppercorns, onions, brown sugar, and caraway seeds. No need to blend. The cooking will combine the elements.

3. COOK on high for 2½–3 hours.

4. WITH half an hour to go, add hotdogs or sausage.

5. PEEL, quarter, and boil potatoes, adding salt, until fork goes in smoothly, about 15–20 minutes. Mash potatoes with butter and ¼ cup milk. Use additional milk to get to desired consistency.

6. SERVE sauerkraut mixture over mound of mashed potatoes.

SERVES
6-8

A MOTHER'S DELIGHT

SERVES 4-6

This is a family staple.

1 LB. GROUND BEEF

2 (10-OZ.) BOXES CHOPPED SPINACH

4 EGGS

SALT AND PEPPER TO TASTE

· · · DIRECTIONS · · ·

1. BROWN ground beef and set aside.

2. THAW and squeeze moisture out of spinach.

3. MIX ground beef and spinach in a frying pan at medium heat.

4. MAKE a well in the spinach/ground beef. Put eggs in the well and mix the spinach, ground beef, and eggs.

5. FRY at medium heat till eggs are done.

6. ADD salt and pepper to taste.

NOTE: This can be served successfully over rice.

SPAGHETTI DINNER

SERVES
4-6

A bold dinner recipe.

1 LB. GROUND BEEF

SALT AND PEPPER TO TASTE

2 CUPS SLICED FRESH MUSHROOMS

½ ONION, DICED

3 TBSP. BUTTER

2 (8-OZ.) CANS TOMATO SAUCE

1 (15-OZ.) CAN DICED ITALIAN TOMATOES

1 PKG. LAWRY'S SPAGHETTI SAUCE MIX

2 CUPS WATER

1 LB. PASTA OF CHOICE

· · · DIRECTIONS · · ·

1. COOK ground beef and crumble into bite-size pieces. Add salt and pepper. Set aside.

2. IN A large saucepan, sauté sliced fresh mushrooms and onions in butter.

3. ADD ground beef, tomato sauce, and diced Italian tomatoes.

4. STIR in package of Lawry's spaghetti sauce mix. Simmer for 15–20 minutes. Add water as needed.

5. PREPARE pasta per directions on page 35.

6. LADLE sauce on top of a generous helping of pasta.

NOTE: There are many great spaghetti recipes available. However, sometimes you're in a hurry to have something really good but have limited time. At these times, a good prepared item, like Lawry's spaghetti sauce, is just what you need.

TORTILLA ESPANOLA

SERVES
6-8

No bullfighter in his right mind would enter the ring without having had this for breakfast.

6 STRIPS BACON, CUT INTO ½-INCH PIECES

1½ CUPS PLUS 2 TBSP. OLIVE OIL

2½ LBS. BOILED POTATOES, PEELED AND CUT INTO ⅓-INCH PIECES

2½ CUPS CHOPPED ONION

1 TBSP. COARSE SALT, DIVIDED

PEPPER TO TASTE

10 LARGE EGGS

· · · DIRECTIONS · · ·

1. COOK bacon until not too crisp in a 12-inch non-stick skillet. Set aside.

2. ADD 1½ cups oil to skillet and heat at moderate temperature until hot but not smoking. Add potatoes, onions, and half of salt. Cook over moderately low heat, stirring occasionally, until potatoes are very tender but not colored, about 45 minutes.

3. DRAIN the potatoes and onions and cool for 5 minutes.

4. LIGHTLY beat eggs in a large bowl. Gently stir in drained potatoes, bacon, and onions with 1 tablespoon oil, remaining salt, and pepper.

5. ADD 1 tablespoon oil to skillet and add mixture, pressing potatoes until even with eggs. Cook over low heat, covered, 12–15 minutes, or until almost set. Turn off heat and let stand, covered, for 15 minutes.

6. SHAKE skillet gently to make sure tortilla is set on bottom and not sticking to skillet.

7. INVERT tortilla onto a large plate and slide back into skillet, bottom side up. Round edge with a rubber spatula and cook over low heat, covered, for 15 more minutes, or until set.

8. SLIDE tortilla onto a serving plate. Slice and serve warm or at room temperature.

BÉCHAMEL SAUCE

This white sauce is versatile.

2 TBSP. BUTTER

1½–2 TBSP. FLOUR

1 CUP MILK

SALT AND PEPPER TO TASTE

PINCH OF NUTMEG

· · · DIRECTIONS · · ·

1. MELT butter over low heat.

2. ADD flour and blend for 3–5 minutes.

3. POUR milk in slowly, stirring constantly. Cook until thickened. Salt and pepper to taste.

4. ADD a pinch of nutmeg. Serve over favorite cooked pasta. Sprinkle with additional nutmeg as desired.

NOTE: Stir in 1½ cups grated cheese and you'll have a sauce to add to cooked macaroni . . . your own mac and cheese!

SERVES
4-6

CHAPTER 11
DESSERTS

"Seize the moment. Remember all those women on the *Titanic* who waved off the dessert cart."

—ERMA BOMBECK

MOM'S CHOCOLATE CHIP COOKIES

This is our family's favorite chocolate chip cookie recipe, and we know what we're talking about.

¾ CUP BROWN SUGAR

¾ CUP WHITE SUGAR

1 CUP BUTTER OR 1 CUP SHORTENING, OR ½ CUP BUTTER AND ½ CUP SHORTENING

1 EGG

1 TSP. BAKING SODA

½ TSP. SALT

1 TSP. VANILLA

2¼–2½ CUPS FLOUR

1–2 CUPS CHOCOLATE CHIPS

1–1½ CUPS NUTS

· · · DIRECTIONS · · ·

1. PREHEAT oven to 375°F.

2. IN A mixing bowl, mix first three ingredients until smooth. Add egg and mix in the remaining ingredients, except chips and nuts.

3. FOLD in chocolate chips and nuts at very slow speed or with a wooden spoon.

4. DROP dough by teaspoonfuls onto cookie sheet.

5. BAKE for 8–10 minutes.

SERVES
6-8

GRANDMA'S CUSTARD

SERVES
6

There wasn't much that grandma made that we didn't like, and there were some things we loved . . . this is one.

6 EGGS

4 CUPS MILK

1 CUP SUGAR

1 TSP. VANILLA

PINCH OF SALT

NUTMEG TO TASTE

· · · DIRECTIONS · · ·

1. FILL a large baking dish or pan halfway with water and place it in the oven at 350°F.

2. IN A mixing bowl, add eggs (including whites and yolks), milk, sugar, vanilla, and a pinch of salt and stir with a wire whisk until smooth, making sure none of the sugar is sticking to the sides or bottom of the bowl.

3. POUR contents into six or seven ramekins. Sprinkle a little nutmeg on top of the liquid custard in each container. Place ramekins into the preheated water in the baking dish and cook 45–60 minutes. The custard is done when you can insert a knife blade that comes out clean, or until the custard top begins to mound. Serve hot or cold. If you have the patience, this custard is better the next day.

TEXAS SHEET CAKE

It may actually be a brownie . . . but who cares?

2 CUPS FLOUR

2 CUPS GRANULATED SUGAR

1 TSP. BAKING SODA

1 LB. BUTTER

1 CUP WATER

4 TBSP. UNSWEETENED COCOA

1 CUP BUTTERMILK

2 EGGS, BEATEN

1 TSP. VANILLA

· · · DIRECTIONS · · ·

1. PREHEAT oven to 400°F.

2. MIX flour, sugar, and baking soda in a mixing bowl.

3. MELT butter and add water and cocoa. Stir until well mixed.

4. BRING cocoa mixture to a boil and pour into flour mixture. Add buttermilk, beaten eggs, and vanilla. This will be a thin batter. Pour into cookie sheet (with high sides). Bake for 25–30 minutes.

5. LET cake cool slightly and pour on frosting (see next page). Both frosting and cake should be warm when icing. Refrigerate for at least 2 hours before serving.

SERVES 15-20

TEXAS SHEET CAKE FROSTING

½ LB. BUTTER

4 TBSP. COCOA

6 TBSP. BUTTERMILK

1 (16-OZ.) BOX POWDERED SUGAR

1 TSP. VANILLA

1 CUP PECANS

· · · DIRECTIONS · · ·

1. MIX first three ingredients in a saucepan and bring to a boil.

2. STIR in remaining ingredients until smooth.

3. POUR frosting on cake.

CHOCOLATE PIE

This pie is a pleasant way to put on a pound or two.

1 PIE CRUST

1 PINT WHIPPING CREAM

½ CUP SUGAR

1 TSP. VANILLA

1 (6.8-OZ.) HERSHEY'S CHOCOLATE BAR WITH ALMONDS

· · · DIRECTIONS · · ·

1. BAKE pie crust per instructions.

2. MAKE whipped cream with whipping cream, sugar, and vanilla per instructions on page 14. Divide whipped cream in half.

3. MICROWAVE chocolate bar for 60 seconds so it's soft but not running. Beware: Chocolate is deceptive. It may not appear to be melted when it is.

4. MIX chocolate and half of whipping cream.

5. POUR mixture into pie crust. Spread remaining whipped cream on top.

6. CHILL for 2 hours before serving.

SERVES
6-8

SUGGESTIONS FOR HOMEMADE ICE CREAM

1. PURCHASE (or borrow) an ice cream maker. An ice cream maker consists of a bucket that holds the canister and ice. The canister holds the ice cream and sits inside the bucket. A dash is a paddle that turns inside the canister so the ice cream is pushed alongside the wall of the canister and freezes. An electric motor sits on top of the canister and turns the dash.

2. SHOULD you buy an electric or hand-crank ice cream maker? Electric! (Walking to New Orleans from Portland versus flying is the same choice.)

3. CHOOSE a maker that is tall and narrow versus wide and short. The narrower canister will freeze faster and more thoroughly.

4. BUY a bag or two of party ice. You'll need more than you have in your typical ice maker. Add ice cubes around outside of canister, and add rock salt (not kitchen salt) every 2 to 3 inches of ice. Do not add water to the ice! Do not let salt get into ice cream, but use plenty of salt.

5. CHECK ice level every 15 minutes or so. Add ice and salt when needed.

PEACH ICE CREAM

SERVES 6-8

See page 113 for more suggestions.

2 (29-OZ.) CANS PEACHES

2 CUPS SUGAR, DIVIDED

1 (6-OZ.) PKG. PEACH JELL-O

¾ TSP. SALT

2 TBSP. VANILLA

ICE CREAM MAKER/FREEZER

2 QTS. WHIPPING CREAM

MILK

1–2 BAGS PARTY ICE

ROCK SALT

· · · **DIRECTIONS** · · ·

1. DRAIN peaches, reserving juice. Add 1 cup sugar and puree.

2. BOIL reserved juice and dissolve peach Jell-O in boiling juice. Let it cool and add to peach puree along with salt and vanilla.

3. POUR mixture into ice cream maker canister. Stir in whipping cream and remaining sugar. Add milk to the fill line indicated on the canister.

4. PUT the dash in the canister with lid. Put the canister in the ice cream maker, attach motor, and plug in. Add ice around canister, about 2 inches at a time. Sprinkle rock salt generously on top of ice. Repeat until the you reach the spill hole on the bucket that holds the canister and ice. Listen to the turning of the ice cream, and when it starts to slow down, the ice cream is done. It will be soft.

5. TO make the ice cream hard/harder, there are two options. One: Remove the canister and remove the dash (so that it won't freeze in the ice cream), put the lid back on the canister, and replace it in the ice. Put a towel on top for insulation and let it sit in the ice for 30 minutes to 1 hour. This allows it to continue to freeze. Two: After having removed the dash, put the canister with lid in your refrigerator freezer, and let it continue to freeze for 30 minutes to 1 hour, or even longer.

STAN FORD SHERBET

My wife and I made this a lot in college.

1 CUP SUGAR

1 CUP MILK

1 CUP HEAVY CREAM

2 LEMONS

· · · DIRECTIONS · · ·

1. BEAT sugar, milk, and cream in a mixing bowl until sugar is dissolved.

2. FREEZE for 6 hours.

3. IN A separate bowl, squeeze the juice of two lemons. Zest the rinds of both lemons and add to the juice.

4. BEAT the juice and zest into the frozen milk dish and refreeze.

SERVES
6

STRAWBERRY ICE CREAM

This was our young family's favorite ice cream. See page 113 for more suggestions.

2 BASKETS STRAWBERRIES

1⅓ CUPS SUGAR, DIVIDED

2 CUPS WHOLE MILK

ICE CREAM MAKER

4 CUPS WHIPPING CREAM

½ CUP FRESH LEMON JUICE

1–2 BAGS PARTY ICE

ROCK SALT

· · · DIRECTIONS · · ·

1. PUREE strawberries with ⅓ cup sugar and milk.

2. POUR pureed mixture into the ice cream maker canister and stir in cream, lemon juice, and the remaining cup of sugar with a long-handled spoon.

3. PUT canister in ice cream maker and freeze per directions given in Peach Ice Cream recipe (page 114).

SERVES
8

ORANGE CHOCOLATE CHIP ICE CREAM

See page 113 for more suggestions.

1 (3-OZ.) PKG. ORANGE JELL-O

½ CUP BOILING WATER

1 CUP ORANGE JUICE CONCENTRATE

2 EGGS

½ CUP SUGAR

1½ QTS. WHIPPING CREAM

½ TSP. VANILLA

ICE CREAM MAKER

1–2 BAGS PARTY ICE

ROCK SALT

¾ CUP CHOCOLATE BITS

· · · DIRECTIONS · · ·

1. DISSOLVE Jell-O in boiling water. Blend in concentrated orange juice. Cool for 15 minutes in refrigerator.

2. BEAT eggs. While beating add sugar until creamy.

3. ADD cream and vanilla to egg mixture.

4. POUR egg mixture and orange mixture into blender. Blend until smooth, not bubbly.

5. POUR mixture into ice cream maker canister and freeze per directions given in Peach Ice Cream recipe (pages 114–15), plus the following: When you remove dash to serve soft ice cream (or prior to additional freezing), pour in chocolate bits and stir. Once thoroughly blended, either serve or allow to harden per Peach Ice Cream directions.

SERVES
8

SUE'S CHOCOLATE ICE CREAM

My wife's recipe—it includes a custard, but it's worth the extra effort. See page 113 for more suggestions.

2 TBSP. CORNSTARCH

5 TBSP. COCOA

1½ CUPS SUGAR

2 CUPS WHOLE MILK

2 EGGS, WHISKED

1 TSP. VANILLA

5 CUPS WHIPPING CREAM

ICE CREAM MAKER

1–2 BAGS PARTY ICE

ROCK SALT

SERVES
8

· · · DIRECTIONS · · ·

1. MIX cornstarch, cocoa, and sugar in a medium saucepan. Gradually add milk. Stir over medium heat, until mixture starts to bubble and thicken.

2. WHISK eggs in a bowl.

3. IN small amounts, add warm milk mixture a little at a time into eggs until the egg solution is warm, about half of the milk mixture.

4. AFTER egg solution is warm, pour into remainder of the milk mixture. Bring to a near boil, where bubbles are forming, and stir in vanilla.

5. REMOVE from stove and let cool. Stir occasionally so that the top doesn't form a hard coat.

6. REFRIGERATE for an hour or so and then pour into ice cream maker canister. Stir in cream and then freeze in your ice cream maker, per directions found in Peach Ice Cream recipe (pages 114–15).

NOTE: You can make vanilla ice cream the same way as above by omitting the cocoa.

CHERRY CHOCOLATE ICE CREAM

There's something about chocolate and cherries. See page 113 for more suggestions.

3 SLIGHTLY BEATEN EGGS

2 CUPS MILK

4 CUPS WHIPPING CREAM

1 CUP SUGAR

1 CUP CHOCOLATE SYRUP

1 (10-OZ.) JAR MARASCHINO CHERRIES, CHOPPED

1 TBSP. VANILLA

½ LARGE HERSHEY'S BAR, GRATED

ICE CREAM MAKER

1–2 BAGS OF PARTY ICE

ROCK SALT

· · · DIRECTIONS · · ·

1. IN A large bowl combine the eggs, milk, whipping cream, sugar, chocolate syrup, chopped cherries, and vanilla. Pour mixture into ice cream maker canister. Freeze per directions found in Peach Ice Cream recipe (pages 114–15). Fold in grated chocolate after frozen and dash is removed.

SERVES
8

CHAPTER 12
DRINKS

These drinks look good and taste even better. They slake the thirst, are fun to drink, and no matter how much you enjoy, you can still drive yourself and your family and friends home.

CRANBERRY JUICE

This is surprisingly refreshing.

64 OZ. CRAN-RASPBERRY JUICE

2 LITERS GINGER ALE

· · · DIRECTIONS · · ·

1. MIX cran-raspberry juice and ginger ale.

MAKES
4 QTS.

PIÑA COLADA

7 OZ. COCONUT MILK

6 OZ. PINEAPPLE JUICE FROZEN CONCENTRATE

⅓ CUP SUGAR

2 CUPS MILK

1 TSP. VANILLA

2 CUPS ICE

· · · DIRECTIONS · · ·

1. COMBINE all ingredients except ice in blender in order.

2. ADD ice slowly while blending. Blend until smooth.

SERVES
4

SPARKLING DINNER WATER

1 CUP LEMON JUICE

5 CUPS ORANGE JUICE

3 TBSP. GRENADINE SYRUP OR MARASCHINO CHERRY JUICE

2½ CUPS SUGAR

3¾ QTS. CHILLED SPARKLING WATER

· · · DIRECTIONS · · ·

1. COMBINE juices and syrup with sugar. Stir to dissolve sugar.

2. ADD sparkling water.

SERVES
10

SUE'S FROZEN PUNCH

This is a hit at a party.

5 BANANAS

6 OZ. FROZEN LEMONADE CONCENTRATE

12 OZ. FROZEN ORANGE JUICE CONCENTRATE

12 OZ. FROZEN PINEAPPLE CONCENTRATE

4 CUPS SUGAR

6 CUPS WATER

8 MARASCHINO CHERRIES, CUT IN HALF

2 LITERS LEMON-LIME SODA

· · · DIRECTIONS · · ·

1. MASH bananas and combine juices, sugar, water, and cherries. Heat over medium heat until sugar is dissolved. Let cool to room temperature. Freeze in large container.

2. ABOUT half an hour before serving, put in punch bowl while frozen and add lemon-lime soda.

3. ALLOW to sit and thaw to form a slush.

SERVES
10-12

AFTERWORD

PUTTING IT ALL TOGETHER

YOU CAN TELL RIGHT AWAY when a spouse helps her husband get dressed. He's stylish and everything is coordinated, but he looks out of place. And this brings up a point about cooking. There are things that "go together" and there are things you like, such as pickles and peanut butter. Since this book is about allowing you to cook what you want and when, the same goes for putting meals together. Try putting dishes together the way you want, and you'll find out pretty soon whether you really like them or not.

HOWEVER, HERE ARE SOME SUGGESTIONS:

- The soups and sandwiches go well together.

- The soups and green salads go well together.

- The sandwiches and salads go well together.

- The meats go well with the side dishes and green salads.

- Ham will work with almost any of the salads and sides.

- The chili meals are largely complete by themselves, except with the addition of corn bread.

- The Mexican recipes are suggested as part of a single meal, served along with the Quick Pork Chili.

- The barbecue dishes go well with the sides and salads.

- Indian Chicken and Rice Tout de Suite is complete, as are Sauerkraut aus Deutschland, Shrimp Louie, and Baked Potato Bar.

- For dessert, make whatever sounds good to you.

- While not included in this book, breads or rolls go well with almost all dishes.

SPICES USED IN *NO GIRLS ALLOWED*:

- baking soda
- basil
- bay leaves
- beef bouillon
- brown sugar
- caraway seeds
- cayenne pepper
- chicken bouillon
- chili powder
- chives
- cinnamon
- cornstarch
- crushed red pepper
- cumin
- dill
- dry mustard
- garlic powder
- granulated sugar
- nutmeg
- olive oil
- onion powder
- oregano
- parsley
- pepper
- peppercorns
- powdered sugar
- restaurant-quality ground pepper
- salt
- thyme
- vanilla
- vinegar
- worcestershire sauce

MEASUREMENT
CONVERSION CHART

16 tablespoons	1 cup
12 tablespoons	¾ cup
10 tablespoons + 2 teaspoons	⅔ cup
8 tablespoons	½ cup
6 tablespoons	⅜ cup
5 tablespoons + 1 teaspoon	⅓ cup
4 tablespoons	¼ cup
2 tablespoons	⅛ cup
2 tablespoons + 2 teaspoons	⅙ cup
1 tablespoon	1/16 cup
2 cups	1 pint
2 pints	1 quart
3 teaspoons	1 tablespoon
48 teaspoons	1 cup

INDEX

ABOUT THE AUTHOR

SOME YEARS AGO, Greg Ford made a recipe book for his son when he got married. It was a good time to collect some of the favorite recipes for men from family and friends and pass them on to him. The book was well received by family members and strangers who bumped into it. And so Greg's writing of recipes began. While some of the recipes survived from that first cookbook, many of the recipes in *No Girls Allowed* are new, collected from the wide array of terrific cooking he has enjoyed during his life.

GOING WAY BACK, Greg was born, grew up, got married, and raised a family in the Bay Area of California. Since then, they spent six years apiece in Austin, Texas (barbecue!), and Delray Beach, Florida. He is a graduate of Stanford University and Stanford Graduate School of Business. Greg's day job was in finance and product management.

GREG AND HIS WIFE now live in Eagle Mountain, Utah. They have five married children and twenty-three grandchildren, all of whom are always hungry and know better than anyone what's in the refrigerator.